CONTENTS

D0320345

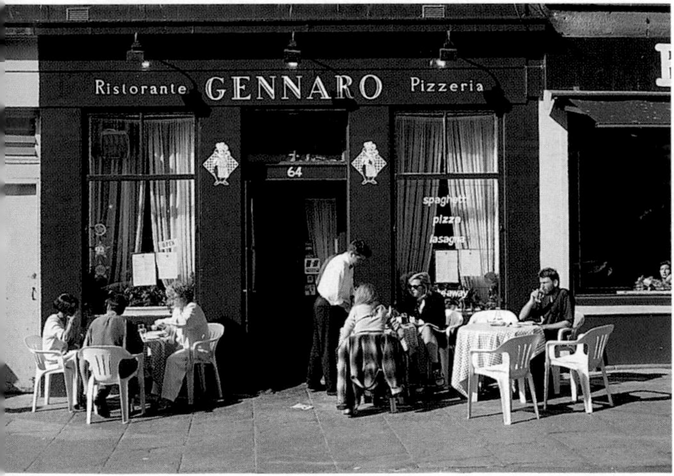

Ristorante GENNARO Pizzeria
64
spaghetti
pizza
lasagna

Edinburgh

THE CITY AND THE PEOPLE

On New Year's Eve a huge bonfire burns on the summit of Calton Hill as the people of Edinburgh celebrate the end of the old year and the start of the new. Hogmanay is a traditional Scottish festival, a time to look back on past achievements whilst turning a shrewd eye towards the year ahead, and Edinburgh, a city steeped in history, is a fitting place to mark the turning of the year.

The past hangs heavy in the narrow streets and alleyways of the Old Town, but nowhere is its presence so strongly felt as within the walls of the castle. The castle is the reason for the city's existence, the focus for the settlement which grew up on the Castle Rock from the 11th century onward. Today the castle is usually the first place that visitors head for when they arrive—it is the city's (and indeed Scotland's) top tourist attraction, drawing over a million visitors a year. Its distinctive silhouette is a symbol of Edinburgh, dominating the city-centre skyline and featuring in countless pictures and postcards.

From the old battlements of the castle's Half-Moon Battery you can look out over five centuries of Edinburgh's history. The 15th-century crown spire of St. Giles rises high among the 16th- and 17th-century Old Town tenements that crowd the Royal Mile. The North Bridge joins the Old Town to the 18th-century Georgian terraces of the New, while the 19th century is represented by the railway lines in the valley of the Nor' Loch, and the two grand railway hotels—the Caledonian and the Balmoral (formerly the North British) —that stand at either end of Princes Street. To the north and south sprawl the 19th- and 20th-century suburbs that lie between the Firth of Forth and the Pentland Hills. There is even history beneath your feet: The Half-Moon Battery stands on the ruins of David's Tower, built for the Scottish king in the 14th century.

The feeling that the past is all around you is one of Edinburgh's great attractions. Another is its spectacular setting, the natural architecture that provides a backdrop for the many lovely buildings. Robert Louis Stevenson, one of Edinburgh's most famous sons, described it as *"... this profusion of eccentricities, this dream in masonry and living rock ...."* Climb the volcanic crags of the Castle Rock, Calton Hill, and Arthur's Seat and you will be rewarded with an endless succession of views—the turreted skyline of the Old Town, spiked with spires; the towering battlements of the castle perched atop their dizzy crag; the hazy outline of the Pentlands, rising to the south; and distant prospects of the sea, with islands floating in the Firth like ships at anchor.

But Edinburgh is no dull, dead monument—it is a living, breathing city. The Old Town closes and New Town terraces in the heart of the city are still in residential use. In a recent survey of the quality of life in British cities, Edinburgh came out as one of the United Kingdom's most desirable locales. Its history and landscape, combined with fine architecture, good shops and restaurants, a wide range of cultural activities, and easy access to the countryside certainly make it an attractive place to stay.

Although Edinburgh was for centuries the seat of Scottish kings and of Scotland's government, no king has ruled here since 1603, and parliament was moved to London in 1707. But it is still the seat of Scottish regional government, and a gigantic new building to house the Scottish Office has just been completed on the waterfront at Leith. The majority of Scots are in favour of greater self-determination and hope that some form of Scottish Parliament will one day return to Edinburgh.

Edinburgh's modern aspirations are further reflected in its building projects. New offices and a huge new conference cen-

The Castle is Edinburgh's top tourist attraction, attracting over one million visitors a year.

tre off Lothian Road mark the city's status as an important European financial centre, while its role at the heart of the Scottish legal system is confirmed in the new law courts above the Cowgate. On the corner of Chambers Street, a fine extension to the Royal Museum of Scotland is being built to house collections that celebrate Scotland's role, both past and present, at the leading edge of research. Edinburgh University, founded in the 16th century, is an internationally recognized centre of excellence, with achievements to its name in medicine, letters, chemistry and artificial intelligence.

The gleaming façade of the new Festival Theatre mirrors the city's continuing commitment to the arts, and its position as the cultural capital of Scotland. The Edinburgh Festival and Fringe, held annually since 1947, is the world's biggest and most diverse arts festival, and draws hundreds of thousands of visitors every year. It has spawned a number of smaller but no less important events, such as the Film Festival, Jazz Festival, Book Festival, and Folk Festival, and recently the Science Festival, Children's Festival, and the Festival of the Environment. Little wonder that Edinburgh is known as the Festival City!

As a visitor, you can revel in both aspects of Edinburgh, exploring the rich history of the castle and the Old Town, and enjoying the modern delights of its charming pubs, restaurants, theatres, and galleries. Unless your sole reason for travelling to Edinburgh is to experience the festival, there is no best time to

see the city, but try if you can to make at least one visit during Hogmanay, and join the crowd around the bonfire on Calton Hill. Look from the ancient silhouette of the castle across the valley to the expectant fire-lit faces waiting for the stroke of midnight, and join with them in celebration of a city proud of its past, but looking resolutely towards the future.

Street entertainers are out in force during the Festival.

A BRIEF HISTORY

The city of Edinburgh grew up around the beetling crag of the Castle Rock and its easily defended summit. Archaeological excavations have revealed evidence of habitation here as long ago as 900 B.C. However, very little is known about the Rock and its inhabitants in the centuries between its first occupation and the time of the MacAlpin kings. A few shadowy details have been left to us by the Romans, and through an epic poem written by a seventh-century bard.

Romans and Britons

The Roman invasion of Britain commenced about 55 B.C. when Julius Caesar crossed the English Channel from newly conquered Gaul. Scotland was invaded in A.D. 78–84 by forces under Agricola, whose campaign was halted north of the Forth by the ferocious resistance of the Picts. The Romans returned north to consolidate their gains around A.D. 142, and built Antonine's Wall across the waist of Scotland between the Firth of Forth and the River Clyde. They also built forts at Inveresk (in Musselburgh) and Cramond (see page 61).

The Roman legions who manned this far-flung outpost of empire found the strongholds of the Castle Rock, Arthur's Seat, and Blackford Hill held by a tribe of ancient Britons whom they came to know as the Votadini. Little is recorded about this people, but they were probably the ancestors of the Gododdin, whose feats are told in an Old Welsh manuscript from the seventh century. The bard Aneirin describes the Gododdin king, Mynyddog Mwynfawr, and his warriors feasting in the "hall of Eidyn," before being defeated in battle against the Angles at Catraeth (now Catterick in Yorkshire).

The "capital" of the Gododdin was Din Eidyn (the "Fort of Eidyn," almost for certain the Castle Rock), whose name lives

The 12th-century Chapel of St. Margaret is Edinburgh's oldest surviving building.

on in the "Edin" of "Edinburgh." Din Eidyn fell to the Angles in 638 and became part of the Anglian kingdom of Northumbria. The stronghold lay on the natural invasion route along the east coast, and this was the first of many occasions on which the fort of Eidyn would change hands between the kingdoms of the north and of the south.

The MacAlpin Kings

Four distinct peoples inhabited the land now known as Scotland—the Picts in the north, the Britons in the southwest, the invading Angles in the southeast, and the Scots in the west. The Scots were Gaelic-speaking immigrants from the north of Ireland who had established a kingdom in what is now Argyll (from Earra Gael, the "Land of the Gael"). Kenneth MacAlpin, who ruled as king of Scots at Dunadd, acquired the Pictish throne in 843 and united Scotland north of the Forth into a single kingdom. He moved his capital, along with the Stone of Destiny (on which Scottish kings were crowned), to the Picts' sacred site of Scone, close to Perth. His great-great-great-grandson, Malcolm II (1005-1034), defeated the Angles at the Battle of Carham in 1018 and extended Scottish territory as far south as the River Tweed. These new lands included the stronghold of Edinburgh.

Malcolm II's own grandson, Malcolm Canmore (1058-1093), and his wife Margaret, a Saxon princess, often visited Edinburgh, crossing the Forth from Dunfermline at the narrows known to this day as Queensferry (see page 69). Margaret was a deeply pious woman (she was subsequently canonized), and her youngest son, David I (1124-1153) founded a church in her name on the highest point of the Castle Rock (St. Margaret's Chapel is still standing today). David also founded the Abbey of Holyrood, and created several royal burghs (towns with special trading privileges) including Edinburgh and Canongate (the latter under the jurisdiction of the monks, or "canons," of Holyrood).

At this time Edinburgh was still a very modest town, overshadowed by the busy port of Berwick, and the royal retreats of Perth and Stirling. But David's successor, Malcolm IV (1153-1165), made the castle here his main residence, and by the end of the 12th century Edinburgh's castle was used as a royal treasury for the safekeeping of the crown jewels and the national records. The town's High Street stretched beneath the castle along the ridge to the east (nowadays the Royal Mile), past the parish church of St. Giles, to the Netherbow (where Edinburgh ended and Canongate began).

In 1286 the MacAlpin dynasty ended with the death of Alexander III. The only surviving heir was his four-year-old granddaughter Margaret, who died in Orkney during the long sea journey to Scotland from her home in Norway.

Wars of Independence

The death of the "Maid of Norway" left Scotland without a ruler. There were a number of claimants to the throne, among them John Balliol, Lord of Galloway, and Robert de Brus, Lord of Annandale. Faced with this choice, the Guardians of Scotland were unable to decide who should

13

succeed, and asked the English king, Edward I, to adjudicate. Edward saw this invitation as a chance to assert his claim as overlord of Scotland, and chose John Balliol, whom he judged to be the weaker character.

Edward treated King John as a vassal, and taunted him relentlessly, summoning him to Westminster on the slightest of pretexts. However, when Edward went to war with France in 1294 and summoned John like any other knight, the Scottish king decided he had had enough. He ignored Edward's summons, and instead negotiated a treaty with the French king, the beginning of a long association between France and Scotland that became known as the "Auld Alliance." Edward was furious.

The English king's reprisal was swift and bloody. In 1296 he led a force of nearly 30,000 men into Scotland, and captured the castles of Roxburgh, Edinburgh, and Stirling. On the way, he sacked the ports of Berwick and Dunbar, slaughtering the townsfolk, burning their houses, and setting his troops free to loot and pillage. The Stone of Destiny, the Scottish crown jewels, and important records were stolen, Scotland's Great Seal was broken up, and the hapless King John was incarcerated in the Tower of London. (The Stone of Destiny was only recently returned—and can now be viewed at Edinburgh Castle). Oaths of fealty were demanded from Scottish nobles, while English soldiers, judges, and officials were installed to oversee the running of the country. Scotland had become little more than an English county.

But the Scots did not take this insult lying down. Bands of rebels, such as those led by William Wallace, began to attack the English garrisons and make harrying raids into English territory. When Wallace was captured, the Scots looked for a new leader and discovered one in Robert the Bruce, grandson of the Robert de Brus rejected by Edward in 1292. Bruce

HISTORICAL LANDMARKS

900 B.C. Late Bronze/early Iron Age: settlement on Castle Rock.

First-second century A.D. Roman occupation of southern part of Scotland. Hill fort of the Votadini tribe on Castle Rock.

A.D. 142-211 Roman fort and harbour at Cramond.

843 Scotland north of the Forth united under Kenneth MacAlpin.

1124-1157 Reign of David I—founds Holyrood Abbey.

1297 Scots rebels under Wallace defeat English at Stirling Bridge.

1314 Scots victory under Robert the Bruce at Bannockburn.

1513 Scots suffer defeat at Flodden. Edinburgh builds city walls.

1544 The Rough Wooing—Henry VIII's forces sack Edinburgh.

1559-1572 John Knox is minister of St. Giles'.

1560 Protestantism is established as Scotland's national faith.

1561-1567 Mary Queen of Scots lives in Holyrood Palace.

1571-1573 The "Lang Siege" badly damages Edinburgh Castle.

1603 Union of the Crowns—James VI of Scotland consequently becomes James I of Great Britain.

1638 The National Covenant is signed at Greyfriars Kirkyard.

1689 William of Orange is invited to take over government of Scotland—civil war between William and Jacobites.

1707 Act of Union and creation of the United Kingdom—Scottish Parliament is dissolved.

1745 Jacobite uprising. Bonnie Prince Charlie's army occupies Holyrood for a brief period.

1767 The building of Edinburgh's New Town begins.

1822 George IV makes his state visit to Edinburgh.

1844 Scott Monument is completed.

1890 Forth Railway Bridge opens.

1947 The first Edinburgh International Festival is held.

1979 Referendum for creation of Scottish Assembly is defeated.

removed his rival, the Red Comyn, by murdering him in Greyfriars Church in Dumfries, an act of sacrilege which earned him excommunication from the Church.

Undeterred, he had himself crowned King of Scots at Scone in 1306, and began his campaign to drive the English out of Scotland. In a series of daring raids, Bruce's men captured many English-held castles and received increasing support from Scottish nobles and churchmen, and from the French king. Edward I died in 1307 and was succeeded by his ineffectual son Edward II, who eventually led an army of some 25,000 men to confront Bruce's army at Bannockburn, near Stirling, in 1314.

The Scots, though outnumbered, gained a famous victory, and sent the English king home "to think again." Robert the Bruce continued to harry the north of England to the point of exhaustion, until the English were forced to sue for peace. A

Fragments of the old city walls recall fear of invasion after the Scots' defeat at Fladden.

truce was called, and a treaty was negotiated at Edinburgh in 1328, ratified by the English parliament a year later as the Treaty of Northampton.

Two of the recurring themes of Scottish history are those of minors inheriting the throne, and of divided loyalties. While many Scottish nobles were dedicated to the cause of independence, others bore grudges against the ruling king and his supporters, or held lands in England, which they feared to lose. These divisions, originating in greed and grievance, and later hardened by religious schism, would forever deny Scotland a truly united voice.

When Robert the Bruce died in 1329, his son and heir, David II, was only five years old. Within a few years the wars with England resumed, aggravated by civil war at home as Edward Balliol (son of John) tried to take the Scottish throne with the help of the English king, Edward III.

The Stewart Dynasty

During these stormy years, the castle of Edinburgh was occupied several times by English garrisons. In 1341 it was taken from the English by William of Douglas, using a cunning ploy—some of his men disguised themselves as porters and merchants delivering supplies to the castle, and dropped their loads at the entrance to stop the gate being closed; the main force poured in through the open gate and slaughtered the English defenders.

In the same year the young David II returned from exile in France and made Edinburgh Castle his principal royal residence, building a tower house on the site of what is now the Half Moon Battery. He died in 1371 and was succeeded by his nephew, Robert II. David's sister Marjory had married Walter the Steward, and their son was the first of the long line of Stewart (later spelled "Stuart") monarchs that would reign over Scotland (and later Great Britain) until the "Glorious Revolution" of 1688.

During the reigns of the first Stewart kings, the strength and wealth of Scotland increased. England was distracted by war with France, and Scottish trade with Europe prospered. New castles were built and new weapons acquired, including the famous gun called "Mons Meg," a gift to James II from the Duke of Burgundy in 1457. Edinburgh emerged as Scotland's main political centre, and was declared by James III (1460-1488) to be "the principal burgh of our kingdom." The Scottish parliament met either in the castle, or in the Tolbooth, a building that sat next to St. Giles' in the High Street.

James IV (1488-1513) confirmed Edinburgh's status as the capital of Scotland by constructing a royal palace at Holyrood. James was famed as a builder of palaces and ships, and as a patron of the arts, rather than as a soldier—in addition to Holy-

The Rough Wooing

Henry VIII was so furious at the Scots for not complying with his plans for a marriage between his son Edward and the infant Mary, Queen of Scots, that he sent an army north to demonstrate to them by force the error of their ways. "Put all to fire and the sword," he ordered his general, the Earl of Hertford. "Burn Edinburgh town, so … as there may remain forever a perpetual memory of the vengeance of God lightened upon the Scots for their falsehood and disobedience." Hertford's campaigns were vicious and bloody—the Abbey of Holyrood was sacked, and parts of Edinburgh were razed to the ground; crops were burned, and the Border abbeys of Jedburgh, Melrose, and Dryburgh were put to the torch. As these attacks were mounted with the intent of securing an Anglo-Scottish royal marriage, the Scots referred to them as "The Rough Wooing."

rood, he built the great halls of Edinburgh and Stirling castles, made considerable additions to the royal palaces of Falkland and Linlithgow, and gave Scotland a navy (its flagship, the 1,000-ton *Great Michael,* was one of the largest warships of its time, far bigger than Henry VIII's 700-ton *Mary Rose*).

He cemented a peace treaty with England by marrying Margaret Tudor, the daughter of Henry VII—the so-called "Marriage of the Thistle and the Rose"—but this did not prevent him from making a raid into England during 1513, which

Henry VIII's matchmaking tactics called for full battle armour.

culminated in the disastrous Battle of Flodden near the banks of the River Tweed. The king, many of his nobles, and thousands of young Scottish soldiers (the "Flowers of the Forest," as they are known in a popular song) all died.

Fearing invasion, the Edinburgh town council built a protective wall around the city (the "Flodden Wall"), enclosing the Grassmarket, Greyfriars, and the south side of the Cowgate—crossing the Royal Mile at the Netherbow Port (nowadays St. Mary's Street). Yet again a minor—the infant James V—succeeded to the throne, and Scots nobles were divided as to whether Scotland should draw closer to England (and avoid a repeat of Flodden), or seek help from her old ally, France. The adult James leant towards France, and in 1537 took a

This carved panel recalls the 1603 Union of the Crowns, when Scotland's James VI became ruler of England as well.

French wife, Mary of Guise. She bore him two sons, who both died in infancy, but by the time she was about to give birth to their third child, her husband lay dying at Falkland Palace. On 8 December 1542, a messenger arrived with news that the queen had been delivered of a daughter at the palace of Linlithgow. Remembering how the Stewart dynasty had begun through Marjory, the grand-daughter of Robert the Bruce (whose son was the first of the Stewart kings), and fearing it would end through lack of a male heir, James murmured "God's will be done. It cam' wi' a lass and it will gang wi' a lass." A few days later he was dead, leaving a week-old baby girl to inherit the Scottish crown.

Mary, Queen of Scots

The baby was Mary Stuart, crowned Queen of Scots at the Chapel Royal, Stirling, at the age of nine months. When the news reached London, Henry VIII saw his chance to bring Scotland under his power, and negotiated a marriage between the infant Mary and his son Edward. As the Scots refused, Henry sent an army rampaging through Scotland on a campaign known as the "Rough Wooing." His death in 1547 brought no respite, since the Earl of Hertford continued his attacks as Edward's regent.

But there was more at stake than Scotland's independence. In order to divorce Catherine of Aragon and marry Anne Boleyn, Henry VIII had broken with Rome and brought the English church under his own control. England became a Protestant country, caught between Catholic France and Scotland and her new Catholic queen. The Scots themselves were divided, many embracing Protestantism in the spirit of the Reformation, while others remained staunchly Catholic. However, fear of the rampaging English army led the Scots again to seek help from their old allies, and the young queen was sent to France to be married to the Dauphin François, the son of the French king.

François II became king of France in 1559, but died soon afterwards, and in 1561 the 18-year-old Mary returned to the Palace of Holyrood, and to a Scotland in the grip of the Reformation. Protestant leaders had taken control of the Scottish parliament—the authority of the pope had been abolished, and the celebration of mass was banned. Her Protestant cousin Elizabeth Tudor was on the English throne, and Elizabeth, the "Virgin Queen," had no heir. Mary, Queen of Scots, was next in line for the English crown, and Elizabeth was suspicious of her intentions.

The six years of Mary's reign were turbulent ones. She clashed early on with Edinburgh's famous Protestant reformer, John Knox, but later adopted an uneasy policy of religious tolerance. In 1565 she married her young cousin

Charles II's reign was one of the most troubled periods in Scotland's history.

Henry, Lord Darnley, at her private chapel in Holyrood, much to the chagrin of her lords, and of Elizabeth (Darnley was a grandson of Margaret Tudor, and thus also had a claim to the English throne). On 19 June, 1566, in the royal apartments in Edinburgh Castle, Mary gave birth to a son, Prince James. The next year, Darnley was murdered, and Mary immersed herself in controversy by marrying the Earl of Bothwell, who was widely held to be the chief suspect.

But the queen's own enemies in Scotland gained the upper hand, and in 1567 Mary was forced to abdicate the Scottish throne. The infant prince was crowned as James VI at Stirling, and Mary sought asylum in England, only to be imprisoned by Elizabeth. The English queen kept her cousin in captivity for 20 years, and finally had her beheaded on a trumped up charge of treason. Yet Elizabeth died without an heir, and James, Mary's son, inherited the English throne.

In 1603, James VI of Scotland rode south to London to be crowned James I of England, marking the Union of the Crowns. While Scotland remained a separate kingdom for the time being, from that day the two countries would be ruled by a single monarch.

The Covenanters

Edinburgh's population grew fast between 1500 and 1650, and a maze of tall, unsanitary tenements sprouted along the spine of the High Street. The castle was extended, and in 1582 the Town's College, the precursor of Edinburgh University, was founded. James died in 1625, and was succeeded by his son, Charles I, who did not come north until 1633, when he was crowned King of Scots at Holyrood. However, Charles was an incompetent and unpopular ruler and he fell afoul of the English parliament as well as provoking dissent in Scotland.

In 1637, Charles's attempt to force the Scottish church to accept an English liturgy and the rule of bishops led to revolt and civil war. When the new form of service was first held in St. Giles', it provoked a riot. The next year, a large group of Scottish churchmen and nobles signed the National Covenant, a declaration condemning the new liturgy and the evils of papistry, and pledging allegiance to the Reformed faith and to Presbyterianism. The Covenanters, as they were called, at first sided with Oliver Cromwell's Parliamentarians in the civil war that had erupted across the border, but

Buried Treasures

The Honours of Scotland—the crown, sword and sceptre of state—were taken from their vault in Edinburgh Castle for the coronation of Charles II at Scone on New Year's Day, 1651. They were then taken to Dunottar Castle near Stonehaven, for fear that they might fall into the hands of Oliver Cromwell's invading forces. When Dunottar was besieged by the English army, the Honours were smuggled out and taken to the manse at nearby Kinneff Church. There the minister hid them at the foot of his bed until he could safely bury them beneath the floor of the church, where they remained for the following nine years. The Regalia were returned to Edinburgh following the Restoration of Charles II in 1660.

when the English revolutionaries beheaded Charles I in 1649, the Scots rallied round his son, Charles II. Cromwell's forces then invaded Scotland, crushed the Covenanter army at the Battle of Dunbar in 1650, and went on to take Edinburgh. Scotland suffered ten years of military rule under Cromwell's Commonwealth.

Scotland's troubles continued after Charles II's restoration to the throne in 1660. The Covenanters faced severe persecution at the hands of the King's supporters (who had decided to follow his father's policy of imposing bishops on the Scots). The Covenanters were forced to meet in secret, and hundreds were imprisoned and executed. An uprising was quashed at the Battle of Rullion Green in the Pentland Hills in 1666. In the end, after England's "Glorious Revolution" of 1688, the Covenanters prevailed. Catholic James VII and II was deposed, the Protestant William of Orange (1689-1702) took the British crown, and Presbyterianism was established as Scotland's official state church.

Act of Union

During the reign of Queen Anne (1702-1713) Scotland and England moved closer towards union—the Scots for economic reasons, the English for security. England threatened the Scots with curtailment of their trading rights and bribed high-ranking members of the Scottish Parliament to speak in favour of union. On 1 May 1707, the two countries were formally joined together by the Act of Union, and the United Kingdom was born. As the members of the Scottish Parliament voted to end that body's independent existence, Lord Seafield murmured, "Now there's an end to an auld sang." But despite the fact that Scotland was allowed to retain its own legal system, its education system, and its national Presbyterian church, the move was opposed by the great majority of Scots.

Several times in the next 40 years the supporters of the deposed James VII and his successors (who were exiled in France), known as the "Jacobites," attempted to restore the Stuart dynasty to the British throne. (The 1701 Act of Settlement decreed that after the death of Anne, who lacked an heir, the British crown should pass to the House of Hanover, a family of German descent). James Edward Stuart, known as the "Old Pretender," was recognized

The New Town, revolutionary in its design for the time.

by Louis XIV of France as King James VIII, and in 1708 he arrived with a French fleet in the Firth of Forth, but was driven back by British ships and bad weather.

Another campaign was held in 1715 under the Jacobite Earl of Mar, but it was the 1745 rising of Prince Charles Edward Stuart, the "Young Pretender," which became the stuff of legend. Bonnie Prince Charlie, the grandson of James VII, raised an army of Jacobite highlanders and swept through Scotland, occupying Perth and Edinburgh (but not the castle), and defeating a government army at the Battle of Prestonpans. In November of that year he invaded England, capturing Carlisle and driving south as far as Derby, only 200 km (130 miles) short of London.

But the young prince found his forces outnumbered and overextended, and he beat a tactical retreat. The British army hounded him all the way back to Scotland, and in the final showdown at Culloden in 1746, the Jacobite army was

Scotland's architectural renaissance led to intellectual growth as well, with a bit of help from Sir Walter Scott.

slaughtered by the troops of the Duke of Cumberland. Not content with this victory, the Duke's army cut down innocent men, women, and children in an orgy of reprisal, earning himself the epithet "Butcher." It was the final land battle of any size to be fought on mainland Britain. Prince Charlie fled, and was pursued over the Highlands for five months, before escaping in a French ship. He died in Rome in 1788, disillusioned and drunk.

The Scottish Enlightenment

The Jacobite risings were very much a Highland movement, however, and they found little support in Lowland cities such as Edinburgh. Here there was a growing sense that the Union was around to stay (despite a bill put before parliament in 1713 that called for its repeal), and a resolve to make the best of a bad situation. Within ten years of the Young Pretender's occupation of Holyrood, Edinburgh's town council proposed a grand plan to relieve the chronic overcrowding of the Royal Mile tenements by constructing a New Town on the ridge to the north of the castle. In 1767, a design by a young and previously unknown architect, James Craig, had been approved, and work began.

Many of the grandest New Town buildings were designed by Robert Adam, whose revival of classical forms swept through Britain and Europe. This architectural renaissance in Edinburgh was followed by an intellectual flowering, when the city played a major role in the advances in science, philosophy, and medicine that revolutionized Western society in the late 18th century. Famous Edinburgh residents of this period—later known as the Scottish Enlightenment—included David Hume, author of *A Treatise of Human Nature*, and one of Britain's greatest philosophers; Adam Smith, author of *The Wealth of Nations,* a pioneer in the study of political economy; and Joseph Black, the scientist who discovered the concept of latent heat.

Robert Burns's poems and Walter Scott's novels rekindled interest in Scotland's history and nationhood, and Scott especially worked hard to raise Scotland's profile. It was he who suggested unearthing the long-forgotten Scottish Honours from their vault inside Edinburgh Castle (see page 23) to set them on public display, and he was largely responsible for organizing King George IV's trip to Edinburgh and Scotland in 1822—the first visit to Scotland by a reigning monarch since the mid-17th century.

The Modern City

In the 19th-century Edinburgh was swept up in the Industrial Revolution, and the coalfields of Lothian and Fife fuelled the growth of baking, distilling, printing, and machine-making industries. With the arrival of the railways in the mid-1800s, the valley of the Nor' Loch was given over for the building of Waverley Station, and new railway lines led to the spread of Victorian suburbs such as Marchmont and Morningside.

The 20th-century saw Edinburgh establish itself as a European centre of learning and culture. Edinburgh University has made outstanding contributions to various fields. The Edinburgh International Festival (held annually since 1947) is acknowledged as one of the world's most important arts festivals. In addition, the city's rich architecture and heritage have made it one of the most popular tourist destinations in the United Kingdom.

Edinburgh has more recently become a focus for political aspirations. A large majority of Scots are in favour of increased self-determination, in the form of a devolved Scottish parliament, or even outright independence. In the 1970s the old Royal High School on Calton Hill was fitted out to provide a debating chamber for a possible Scottish parliament—it could happen that the city that once lay at the political heart of Scotland will again be the capital of a revived Scottish nation.

Sir Walter Scott

Sir Walter Scott (1771-1832) is one of Scotland's most famous and best-loved writers. He was born and educated in Edinburgh, and studied law, but his greatest passion was Scotland's history. He was the inventor, and some would say the greatest exponent, of the historical novel, and his prolific writing career produced many of the classics of the genre, such as Rob Roy, The Heart of Midlothian, Ivanhoe, and Redgauntlet. He lived in George Square and Castle Street in the New Town, before buying a farm in the Borders near Galashiels, where he built his country home, Abbotsford (see page 82).

WHERE TO GO

Edinburgh is a compact city, best explored on foot. The Old Town extends along a ridge, about a mile in length, strung between the castle and the Palace of Holyroodhouse, with the Grassmarket and Greyfriars to the south, and Princes Street Gardens and the New Town to the north.

OLD TOWN

Edinburgh's dramatic contours were moulded by the action of fire and ice. The Castle Rock and Arthur's Seat are deeply eroded stumps of ancient volcanoes, the frozen feeder pipes for lava flows that erupted around 340 million years ago. During the last Ice Age (some 13,000 to 20,000 years ago), massive glaciers flowed from west to east, gouging hollows to either side of the Castle Rock. Like a boulder in a stream, the resistant basalt plug protected the softer sediments downstream, creating a long ridge extending to the east, a feature known to geologists as a "crag-and-tail."

The Old Town of Edinburgh grew up on the "tail" of the Castle Rock's crag. The town had its origins in the settlement that clustered beneath the walls of the early castle, and as its population grew it spread along the crest of the ridge, confined by the steep slopes to either side. By the 16th century, the lack of room to expand sideways had led the citizens to build upwards, and the famous Old Town tenements appeared, lining the High Street five or six stories high, separated by narrow alleys called "closes" or "wynds." The hollow to the south of the Rock was occupied by the Grassmarket, while the one to the north contained a marshy lake called Nor' Loch (now drained and covered by Princes Street Gardens and the railway).

To explore the Old Town fully takes at least a couple of days, but if time is limited you can see the major sights in a single day, starting in the castle, then taking a stroll down the Royal Mile to finish at Holyrood.

The Castle

The Castle Rock's natural defensive position must have attracted settlers from the time humans first arrived in central Scotland. Archaeological excavations have revealed evidence of habitation on the Rock as long ago as 900 B.C., and by the time the Romans arrived in the first century A.D. there was a thriving hill fort occupied by a tribe of ancient Britons called the Votadini.

However, it was King Malcolm Canmore (1057-1093) and his queen, Margaret, who first used Edinburgh's fortified crag as a royal residence. Their youngest son, David I (1124-1153), founded Holyrood Abbey, and constructed the oldest surviving building on the Rock, the tiny chapel dedicated to his mother. During the reigns of David and his successors, Edinburgh Castle assumed increasing importance as a royal stronghold, and played an important part in the bitter Wars of Independence against England. David II (1329-1371), the son of Robert the Bruce, built a massive tower house at the eastern end of the Rock, to strengthen the defences and to provide royal apartments for himself and his queen, and in the 15th century a separate block was added to its south side — the beginnings of the Royal Palace.

The castle suffered heavy damage during the Lang Siege (1571-1573) as supporters of the exiled Mary Queen of Scots, led by Sir William Kirkcaldy of Grange, strove to hold out against the forces of James Douglas, Earl of Morton (Regent of the infant James VI). After a long stalemate Douglas sought assistance from Elizabeth I, and the English artillery unleashed a devastating barrage that flattened David's Tower and most of the walls. Following Kirkcaldy's surren-

Edinburgh Highlights

Arthur's Seat. Edinburgh's own miniature mountain, providing a breath of country air in the heart of the city. Invigorating walks and fine views along the network of footpaths criss-crossing its slopes. Open dawn to dusk. (See page 50)

Charlotte Square. Robert Adam's masterpiece and Britain's finest example of Georgian architecture. Georgian House museum, featuring rooms decorated with period furniture. Open 10:00 A.M.-5:00 P.M. (2:00 A.M.-5:00 P.M. on Sunday). (Closed 1 November-27 March). Adults £3.00, children £1.50. (See page 57)

Cramond. Picture-postcard village on site of ancient Roman harbour. Lovely walks along riverside and coast. (See page 61)

Edinburgh Castle. Historic stronghold, dominating the skyline of Edinburgh. Scotland's most popular tourist attraction. Open daily 9:30 A.M.–5:00 P.M. (April–September), 9:30 A.M.–5:00 P.M. (October–March). Adults £6.00, children £1.50 under 16. (See page 30)

Edinburgh International Festival. The world's biggest and liveliest arts festival, running for three weeks every summer (last two weeks in August and first in September). (See page 83)

Edinburgh Zoo. Famous for its white rhinos and Europe's largest colony of penguins. Penguin parade daily at 2:00 p.m. In summer. Open 9:00 A.M.–6:00 P.M. (from 9:30 A.M. on Sunday; closes 4:30 P.M. October–March). Adults £5.80, children £2.50. (See page 68)

Palace of Holyroodhouse. The Queen's official residence in Scotland. Tours through historic royal apartments, including Mary Queen of Scots' chambers. Open 9:30 A.M.–5:15 P.M. Tuesday–Sunday, 9:30 A.M.–3:45 P.M. Monday. Adults £5.30, under 17 £2.60. The palace is open 7 days a week, all year.

Queensferry. Harbour village set between the spectacular Forth Road and Railway Bridges. Boat trips to beautiful Inchcolm Island with its ruined abbey and seal colony. Deep Sea World at north end of Road Bridge, open April–October 10:00 A.M.–6:00 P.M.; July–August open until 6:30 P.M.; November–March 11:00 A.M.–5:00 P.M. Adults £5.80, children £3.25.

der, new eastern defences were built, and the palace was repaired and extended.

Two other long sieges took place, both of which resulted in repairs and extensions to the fortifications. One was during Cromwell's invasion of Scotland in 1650, when the castle surrendered after three months and was subsequently manned by an English garrison until the restoration of Charles II ten years later. The second occurred in 1689, when the Duke of Gordon defended the castle in the name of the exiled James VI against the forces of William of Orange.

Castle Rock boasts a defensive position that has drawn settlers since 900 B.C.

The Jacobite Rising of 1715 prompted the construction of stronger artillery defences, but a half-hearted attack by Bonnie Prince Charlie's men thirty years later was the last time the castle saw military action. In the 18th and 19th-centuries Edinburgh Castle housed the principal garrison in Scotland, but when the army moved to Redford Barracks after World War I, it was seen more as an ancient monument and tourist attraction. Today, Edinburgh Castle is Scotland's largest tourist attraction, drawing in over one million visitors a year.

At the top of Castlehill you emerge into the open space of the **Esplanade,** beneath the castle's eastern fortifications. A

The Coats-of-Arms of Scottish kings colour the windows of the castle's Great Hall.

parade ground was first created here in 1753, on the bare ridge between town and fortress, but the walled enclosure you see now did not take shape until 1820. You enter the castle proper through a 19th century gatehouse, flanked by statues of William Wallace and Robert the Bruce. A cobbled road then leads uphill through the 16th-century **Portcullis Gate,** built following the Lang Siege (the upper section, above the Lion Rampant, was added in 1886-1887) to the Argyle Battery, with its row of 18-pound cannons. Ahead, to the right of the restaurant, you'll see the Mills Mount Battery, which holds a single, World War II 25-pounder—Edinburgh's famous **One O'Clock Gun.**

The road curves to the left, passing through **Foog's Gate** to the top of the Castle Rock. The original buildings inhabited by Malcolm Canmore and David II were confined to this upper part of the rock, and until the expansion of the fortifications in the 17th and 18th-centuries, Foog's Gate was the main entrance to the fortress. The highest point is occupied by **St. Margaret's Chapel,** the oldest surviving roofed building in Edinburgh, probably built by David I (1124-1153) and dedicated to his mother, Queen Margaret. It fell into disuse and ended up serving as a storehouse and magazine until it was restored in the 19th century. The chancel arch, decorated with a chevron pattern, is original; the five tiny stained-glass windows, portraying St. Andrew, St. Columba, St. Ninian, St. Margaret, and William Wallace, were added in the 1920s. (Look over the parapet opposite the chapel entrance to catch a glimpse of a semicircular grass terrace, lined with minute tombstones—a cemetery for officers' dogs.)

Beyond the chapel you'll find the **Forewall and Half-Moon Batteries,** erected in the 16th century to strengthen the castle's eastern defences after the damage wrought during the Lang Siege of 1571-1573. The site of the Half-Moon Battery used to belong to David's Tower, built in 1367-1368 for David II, but destroyed in the siege. Parts of the 14th-century walls remain in the cellars beneath the battery.

The arch behind the battery leads into **Crown Square,** the main quadrangle of the old castle. On the left side is the

The One O'Clock Gun

Every day (except Sunday) since 1861 a gun has been fired from the ramparts of the castle at exactly 1:00 P.M., as a time signal. It was originally connected to the time ball on the Nelson Monument, which was dropped each day at 1:00 P.M. sharp so that ships anchored in the Forth could check their chronometers. Today it is simply a tradition, but it helps you to tell the locals from the visitors in the Princes Street crowd—when the One O'Clock Gun lets rip, seasoned Edinburghers simply check their watches, while tourists jump about a foot in the air.

Visitors to Edinburgh tend to jump at their first experience of the One O'Clock Gun.

Royal Palace, parts of which date from the 15th and 16th centuries, although it was extensively altered and restored for James VI's homecoming in 1617. The main section houses a fine exhibition on the history of the **Honours of Scotland** (the Scottish Crown Jewels), culminating in a dark, wood-panelled strongroom where the Regalia are displayed.

The Honours of Scotland are the oldest surviving regalia in Europe. The crown was made for James V in 1540, possibly using the gold from the coronet commissioned by Robert the Bruce in 1314, while the Sword of State was a gift given to James IV by Pope Julius II in 1507; the sceptre was also a papal gift, presented in 1494. When the Scottish Parliament was dissolved following the Act of Union in 1707, the Honours were put in a wooden chest in the strongroom, and the room was sealed up. There they lay forgotten until February 1818, when, at the instigation of the novelist Walter Scott, the room was opened and the chest broken into. The Honours were found just as they had been left over a hundred years before; they first went on public display in July 1818 (see page 27).

The **Historic Apartments** in the south part of the palace include the bedchamber of Mary Queen of Scots, and the small cabinet where she gave birth to James VI on 19 June 1566. The cabinet was decorated for James's homecoming in 1617 — the ceiling bears the initials of James and his mother ("IR" for *Iacobus Rex*, "MR" for *Maria Regina*), while on the wall are the Royal Coat of Arms and a verse asking God's blessing for the king.

The square, formerly known as the Palace Yard, occupies an artificial terrace supported by a series of huge vaults resting on the steeply sloping south side of the Castle Rock. The 15th-century vaults provided a foundation for the **Great Hall,** built during the reign of James IV (1488-1513) as a ceremonial setting for royal banquets and sessions of Parliament. The hall was later used as an army barracks and a hospital, before being renovated in 1887-1891. The present interior, which houses a display of weapons on loan from the Tower of London, is entirely 19th-century, except for the splendid hammerbeam roof. This masterpiece of 16th-century timber technology rests on stone corbels (small projecting blocks) decorated with painted carvings: "IR4" with a crown above, for James IV; the Lion Rampant; the Fleur de Lys, recalling the "Auld Alliance" with France; and a vase containing two thistles and a rose, symbolizing the marriage of James IV and the English princess Margaret Tudor.

Across from the Great Hall is the **Scottish National War Memorial** — remodelled from an 18th-century barracks in 1925-1927. Bronze friezes, regimental plaques and stained glass commemorate the Scots who died in the Great War of 1914-1918, and in World War II, while the shrine in the apse contains a steel casket bearing the Scottish Roll of Honour.

Return through Foog's Gate and go down to the left to the entrance to the **Castle Vaults,** some 15th-century stonework chambers underneath Crown Square. These old vaults have a varied history, having seen service as storerooms, barracks, bakery, and prison. Most famously, they were used to hold prisoners of war—many of whom left their mark in the form of graffiti carved in the masonry and woodwork. One of the vaults currently houses **Mons Meg,** one of a pair of enormous siege guns given to James II in 1457. The gun, called a "bombard," was made at Mons (in Belgium) in 1449; it weighs over six tonnes, has a calibre of 50 cm (20 inches), and fired stone cannonballs weighing 150 kg (330lb) for a distance of almost three kilometers (two miles). Its career came to an end in 1681 when the barrel burst while firing a salute—you can see the damaged part just forward of the breech.

The rest of the castle dates mainly from the 18th and 19th centuries, when it served as a military barracks. Most of the buildings are in use and not open to the public. Those that are open include the **Military Prison,** opposite the entrance to the vaults, built in 1842 to hold offenders from the castle garrison; and the ordnance storehouse and hospital, down the road beside the restaurant, now home to the **Scottish United Services Museum.**

The Royal Mile

The Old Town's most famous street, known since the 16th century as the Royal Mile, runs downhill from the Castle Esplanade as far as Holyrood Palace. It was described by the novelist Daniel Defoe in the 1720s as "perhaps, the largest, longest, and finest street, for buildings, and number of inhabitants, in the world."

The Royal Mile is lined with 17th and 18th-century tenements called "lands," rising to six or seven stories above the street, and in olden times to twelve or thirteen stories at the rear. Occasional collapses or fires meant that new buildings were raised on the ruins of the old, and thus the Old Town grew haphazardly, the houses varying in height and appearance, with windows of different sizes and spacing, giving the Royal Mile its distinctive, crowded, hotchpotch character. In the 18th and 19th centuries old tenements behind the street front were pulled down to create open courtyards, allowing light and air into the crowded lands — fine examples are James Court and Milne's Court on the north side of the Lawnmarket.

The Royal Mile acquired its name in the 16th century when it was used by royalty travelling between the castle and the palace. It comprises four parts with separate names, reflecting the historical development of the street — Castlehill; the short Lawnmarket; the High Street, which stretches from George IV Bridge to St. Mary's Street; and the Canongate.

Castlehill

Castlehill is a cobbled ravine leading down the Royal Mile from the Esplanade, flanked by the towering 74-metre (240-foot) spire of the Tolbooth Kirk.

Overlooking the Esplanade are the towers and turrets of **Ramsay Garden,** built in the 1890s around the quaint, octagonal Ramsay Lodge, the 18th-century home of the poet Allan Ramsay. Across the way is the 17th-century **Cannonball House,** so-called because of a cannonball set high in the wall facing the castle. The ball marks the gravitation height of the city's first piped water supply (i.e. the maximum height at which water would flow from a tap under the influence of gravity). The rectangle of masonry below Ramsay Garden is another legacy of Edinburgh's water engineers, as it encloses Castlehill Reservoir. At the upper end is a bronze drinking fountain, the **Witches Well,** with a memorial for the hundreds of women who were burned as witches near this spot between 1479 and 1722.

Also here is the **Outlook Tower,** from where you can observe the city through the **Camera Obscura.** The latter was built during the 1850s; its lenses and mirrors project a live image of the city onto a screen, while a guide recounts the story of Edinburgh. There are displays on lasers, holography, and pinhole photography, and fine views from the tower.

Opposite stands the **Scotch Whisky Heritage Centre,** illustrating the whisky-making process from malting the barley to maturing the spirit in oak casks; a free dram is offered to adult visitors at the end of the trip.

Lawnmarket

The Lawnmarket is the stretch of street between the Tolbooth Kirk and George IV Bridge, and was once the centre of the city's linen trade—hence the name. On the left you will find Gladstone's Land, a typical six-storey Old Town tenement that has been restored by the National Trust for Scotland. It retains painted wooden ceilings, and has been furnished in period style to give visitors a glimpse of 17th-century life in Edinburgh. You will see how people of widely varying social class lived in the same building, with

The narrow streets of the Old Town are lined with colourful shops.

wealthy merchants on the first and second floors, a shop on street level, and poorer people in the upper floors and attic.

Three of Scotland's most famous literary figures are celebrated together in the **Writers' Museum,** which you can find tucked away in Lady Stair's Close. Manuscripts, pictures, letters, and assorted memorabilia relating to Robert Burns, Robert Louis Stevenson, and Sir Walter Scott are displayed in this former home of Elizabeth, Dowager Countess of Stair. Stevenson in particular was influenced by the exploits of one of Edinburgh's more notorious 18th-century characters (see page 45), who is himself commemorated in the pub on the corner called **Deacon Brodie's.** Brodie used to live across the street, just down Brodie's Close (the site of his house is now occupied by a modern office block).

High Street

At the top of the High Street is Parliament Square, the heart of the Old Town, dominated by the crown spire of **St. Giles' Cathedral.** Strictly speaking, this is the High Kirk of Edinburgh; it served as a true cathedral (i.e., the seat of a bishop) only for two periods, 1633-1638 and 1661-1689, before the office of bishop was abolished in Scotland. The first church on this site was probably built in the 12th century, and during the Middle Ages was the only parish church in Edinburgh. It was completely rebuilt in the 15th century, and extensively altered and restored in the 19th; the tower, with its crenellated crown, dates from 1495.

As the principal church of Edinburgh, St. Giles' played a major role in Scotland's ecclesiastical history. The great reformer, John Knox, served as minister here during 1559-1572, and it was here that the Bishop of Edinburgh made his attempt to introduce Charles I's *Book of Common Prayer* in 1637, causing a riot. In 1643, the Solemn League and

Covenant (which sealed Scotland's alliance with the English Parliamentarians against Charles I) was signed here.

The **Thistle Chapel,** in the far right-hand corner of the church, was added in 1909-1911 to serve as the chapel for the Knights of the Thistle. The Most Ancient and Most Noble Order of the Thistle was founded by King James VII and II in 1687, and is the highest order of chivalry in Scotland. There are 16 knights in addition to the reigning monarch, and they attend a service in the chapel each year on the Sunday following St. Andrew's Day (30 November). The interior is in Gothic style, with a high groined ceiling and richly carved oak stalls. To the right of the door is a charming little angel playing bagpipes.

Outside the door of St. Giles', a heart-shaped arrangement of cobblestones marks the site of the Old Tolbooth, which was demolished in 1817 along with a row of timber-fronted tenements and shops (known as the Luckenbooths) that obstructed the High Street beside the church. Since the 16th

Gardyloo!

The Old Town of the 16th–18th centuries was an unsanitary, malodorous, and overcrowded place. Water had to be collected from a street well and carried up six or seven flights of stairs. There were no sewers, simply ditches at the sides of the street to carry away the waste. Those who lived in the upper storeys of the tenements would throw their slops out of the window with a cry of "Gardyloo!" (from the French Garde de l'eau!, "Beware of the water!"). The novelist Daniel Defoe, visiting Edinburgh in the early 18th century, wrote: "In a Morning, earlier than seven o'Clock, before the human Excrements are swept away from the doors, it stinks intolerably; for, after Ten at Night, you run a great Risque, if you walk the Streets, of having Chamber-pots of Ordure thrown upon your Head."

century, the Tolbooth had served as a multi-purpose public building—a place for Parliament to meet, a court of law, a town hall, a church assembly, and notoriously, a prison and place of execution. It was in this latter role that the Tolbooth was immortalized in Sir Walter Scott's novel *The Heart of Midlothian*. When it was finally razed, Scott acquired the door through which condemned prisoners were led to their death, and installed it in his Abbotsford house (see page 82).

An early 19th-century Neoclassical façade around the south side of the square conceals the Law Courts. In the centre is **Parliament House,** built in 1632-1640 to provide a permanent home for the Scottish Parliament, which previously had met in the Tolbooth or in the castle. After the Act of Union, the Scottish Parliament was dissolved; now the 17th-century hall, with its fine hammerbeam roof, serves as a concourse. A splendid stained-glass window in the south wall shows James V inaugurating the Court of Session in 1532.

At the far end of St. Giles' is Edinburgh's **Mercat Cross,** a copy of the 15th-century original. It was once the hub of the Old Town, where people gathered to hear the proclamations of the Lord Lyon, King of Arms. Across the way is the arcaded courtyard of the **City Chambers** (Town Hall), built in 1761 as a Royal Exchange for Edinburgh's merchants, but taken over by the Town Council in 1811. It is only four storeys high on this side, but at the back it plunges 12 stories down to Cockburn Street. The lower part conceals the intact remains of some early 16th-century houses in the old Mary King's Close (guided tours by appointment only).

Downhill from the Chambers is **Anchor Close**—once home to the printing works of William Smellie, editor and printer of the first edition of the *Encyclopaedia Britannica* (1768). Smellie also founded a famous drinking club, known as the "Crochallan Fencibles," based in the local Anchor Tavern (long disappeared), whose members included such notable figures as Adam Smith and Robert Burns.

Beyond the junction with the Bridges, the High Street is constricted by the projecting bulk of **John Knox House.** This 16th-century house belonged to James Mosman, the royal gold smith, who made the Scottish Crown for James V in 1540, but Knox may have lived here during 1561-1572. It is now a museum dedicated to John Knox, with displays of his works and other memorabilia. The

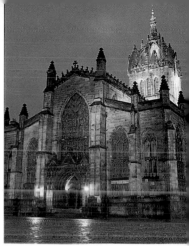

The High Kirk is dedicated to St. Giles, the patron saint of beggars and cripples.

second floor has a fine painted wooden ceiling, and a wall-painting of Cain and Abel, both dating from the 17th century. The outside corner of the building bears a sundial with a figure of Moses pointing at the sun. Across the street stands the **Museum of Childhood.**

At the intersection of the Royal Mile and St. Mary's Street, brass plates in the road show the location of the 16th-century Netherbow Port, the gate that marked the boundary between Edinburgh and the Burgh of Canongate. It was demolished in 1764, but you can see a replica in the Huntly House Museum.

Canongate

Once the residential quarter of the aristocracy, Canongate remained a separate burgh under the jurisdiction of the canons

The Tolbooth Clock in the Canongate is a prominent Royal Mile landmark.

of Holyrood Abbey until it was absorbed into Edinburgh in 1856. A relic of its independence is the old **Canongate Tolbooth,** with its distinctive clock jutting out high above the street. Built in 1591, the Tolbooth was the civic centre of Canongate, serving as town hall, courthouse, and prison. Today it houses **The People's Story,** a museum detailing the life and work of Edinburgh's ordinary folk from the late 18th century to the present.

Opposite the Tolbooth is **Huntly House,** a 16th-century mansion that was restored in 1926-1932 and is now a museum chronicling the history of Edinburgh. Among its fascinating exhibits are an original copy of the National Covenant, a model of Edinburgh as it appeared in the 16th century, and a fine collection of Edinburgh silver, glass, and pottery.

Downhill on the left is the high gable of the 17th-century **Canongate Kirk.** In its kirkyard are buried Mrs. Agnes Maclehose (the "Clarinda" of Burns's love poems), the political economist Adam Smith, and the poet Robert Fergusson. Fergusson died in an insane asylum in 1774, at the age of only 24, but his work had great influence on Robert Burns, who erected a headstone over his pauper's grave in 1787. The epitaph was written by Burns:

> *No sculptured Marble here nor pompous lay,*
> *No storied Urn, nor animated Bust*
> *This simple Stone directs Pale Scotia's way*
> *To pour her Sorrows o'er her Poet's Dust.*

At the very foot of the Royal Mile is **Whitehorse Close,** whose 17th-century buildings have been converted to private flats. This was the site of the White Horse Inn, where Bonnie Prince Charlie's soldiers stationed themselves in 1745, and which was the terminus for the stage-coach to London.

Holyrood

The final fifty yards of the Royal Mile is known as Abbey Strand, and comes to an end before the gates of the **Palace of Holyroodhouse,** the official residence in Scotland of Her Majesty the Queen. The palace was the home of Mary Queen of Scots from 1561-1567, and it was briefly occupied by Bonnie Prince Charlie in 1745. (See page 60 for opening times.)

A Jekyll-and-Hyde Character

Deacon William Brodie was a successful cabinetmaker and locksmith in 18th-century Edinburgh. He was a respectable businessman by day, but at night he secretly pursued a life of gambling, attending cockfights, visiting mistresses, and fathering five illegitimate children. To finance his nocturnal pursuits he took to burglary. During his daily business, he made impressions of shopkeepers' keys in a piece of putty hidden in the palm of his hand; then he paid a blacksmith to make copies, and at night he would rob his fellow tradesmen. He was caught in 1788 after attempting to rob the Excise Office in Chessels's Court, and was hung at the Tolbooth before a huge crowd. Ironically, he himself had designed improvements to the very gallows used for his execution. Deacon Brodie's notorious double life is said to have been the inspiration for Robert Louis Stevenson's story, *The Strange Case of Dr. Jekyll and Mr. Hyde.*

The Abbey of Holyrood was founded by David I in 1128, taking its name from a relic of the True Cross ("rood" means "cross") which had belonged to St. Margaret, David's mother. Another story claims that a cross magically appeared between the antlers of a stag that attacked King David during a hunt—in thanks, the king founded the abbey on the spot where the cross materialized.

David installed a community of Augustinian canons, who built a fine abbey church. The abbey kept a strong royal connection, since the grounds around Arthur's Seat were a favourite hunting ground with the king and his court. The abbey guest house served as a royal residence until the reigns of James IV and James V, when plans were laid for a palace proper, in the form of a quadrangle to the south of the abbey. In 1529-1532 James V built a tower house for himself and his queen, the French princess Mary of Guise, at the northwest

corner of the square, and apartments along the west.

Mary Queen of Scots spent six turbulent years living inside her father's tower, and her son James VI had his queen crowned here in 1590, but after the Union of the Crowns in 1603, the palace lay neglected. It was further enlarged in the 1670s, during the reign of Charles II, when a matching tower was added

Holyrood Palace closes for a few weeks each year when the Queen is staying there.

at the southwest corner, and the other sides of the quadrangle were completed. Charles never saw Holyrood, but his Catholic heir, James VII and II, lived at the palace in the 1680s, and had the nave of the abbey church converted to a Chapel Royal for the benefit of the Knights of the Thistle (destroyed by the mob during the revolution of 1688-1689).

Throughout the 18th century Holyroodhouse was forgotten by the kings and queens of the United Kingdom, comfortably ensconced in London. The palace was neglected, but continued to be used by various noble families. It was not until the visit to Scotland of George IV in 1822 that royal interest began to revive, and during the 19th and 20th centuries much repair and restoration work took place, resulting in the palace you see today. The impressive wrought-iron gates at the north and south ends of the forecourt were erected in 1920-1922 as a memorial to Edward VII. The ornate fountain is an 1859 copy of the one at Linlithgow (see page 75).

The guided tour of Holyrood Palace takes you through the 17th-century royal apartments on the first floor, and into James V's tower house, with the apartments of Mary Queen of Scots and her husband, Lord Darnley, before departing through the ruins of the abbey. The tour begins at the **Great Stair,** the formal approach to the royal apartments. The wonderful plaster ceiling dates from 1678-1679, and depicts four angels bearing a crown, sceptre, sword, and laurel wreath. The walls are hung with paintings and some 16th-century tapestries from Brussels. At the top of the stair, on the left, is the **Royal Dining Room,** which is still used for royal parties. At the far end is a portrait of George IV in highland dress during his visit of 1822, while on the left wall are paintings of Bonnie Prince Charlie and his brother, Prince Henry. Above the fireplace is a copy of the earliest known painting of a clan chief in full highland dress, from 1680 (the original

St. Anthony's Chapel ruins can be explored on the way to the top of Arthur's Seat.

is in the National Portrait Gallery, see page 56).

You now enter the **Throne Room,** the first in the series of apartments made for Charles II during the 17th century. This was originally a guard room, designed to prevent unwanted visitors entering the chambers beyond, but it was used as a throne room for the visit of George IV, and the thrones used by George V and Queen Mary in 1927 are still on view.

The following two rooms, the **Evening and Morning Drawing Rooms,** were built as the king's presence chambers, where he would meet visiting ambassadors. The inner Privy Chamber (the Morning Drawing Room) is perhaps the most beautiful in the palace, with an ornate plaster ceiling and original 17th-century oak panelling. The carved overmantel has a painting of Cupid and Psyche by the Dutch artist Jacob de Wet the Younger; considered too immodest for Queen Victoria's sensibilities, this was covered with a mirror during her reign. The fine Indian carpet is new.

Next door is the more intimate **AnteChamber,** where the king entertained favoured guests; beyond lies the **King's Bed Chamber,** the most opulent of the apartments. Adorning its walls are 17th-century tapestries representing scenes from the life of Alexander the Great, while an oval painting on the ceiling has Hercules being welcomed by the gods atop

Olympus. The bed itself was never used by royalty — it dates from the 1680s and belonged to the Dukes of Hamilton, the Hereditary Keepers of the Palace. It has been extensively restored, but the headboard and canopy are original.

The final chamber is the **King's Closet,** a private study where only the king's closest cronies would be allowed, to drink, smoke, and play cards. You emerge into the **Great Gallery,** a long room lined with portraits of 89 Scottish kings, from the imaginary Fergus (a supposed descendant of Scota, the Pharaoh's daughter who found Moses among the reeds in the Old Testament story), to James VII and II, all painted by Jacob de Wet.

At the far end you pass into the 16th-century **tower house** of James V, with its thicker walls. These first-floor rooms formed part of the queen's apartments following Charles II's remodelling — the ceilings were raised and the windows were enlarged, to make the rooms brighter — and were occupied by the wife of James VII and II in 1679–82, while he was still heir to the throne. The bedchamber boasts a 17th-century bed (encased in glass).

Rizzio's Murder

On a Saturday evening in March 1566, Mary Queen of Scots and her close companions sat down to dinner in the little cabinet that opened off her bedchamber. One of the group was her Italian secretary and favourite, David Rizzio, of whom the queen's husband, Lord Darnley, had become intensely jealous. The dinner was rudely interrupted by the arrival of Darnley and some of his supporters. Darnley restrained the queen (then six months pregnant) while the others "dragged David with great cruelty forth from our cabinet and at the entrance of our chamber dealt him 56 dagger wounds." A brass plaque on the floor marks the spot where he was dumped and left to die.

In the 1560s, these rooms were occupied by Henry, Lord Darnley, the husband of Mary Queen of Scots. Private stairs lead up from the cabinet adjoining his bedroom to **Mary Queen of Scots' Bed Chamber,** the most famous part of the palace. They originally climbed straight up within the thickness of the wall to emerge in a corner (the guide will draw back a tapestry to show you where), but have since been blocked off and replaced by a spiral staircase. From the original corner stair Darnley and his henchmen appeared on the night Mary's Italian secretary, Rizzio, was killed (see page 49). The room has been much altered since Mary last slept in it, but the original wooden ceiling remains, embellished for James VI's homecoming in 1617 with the initials of himself and his mother.

The neighbouring room is **Mary Queen of Scots' Outer Chamber,** where she conducted her famous debates with John Knox, and where Rizzio was left to die. The ceiling is decorated with plaques celebrating Mary's first marriage to the Dauphin François, and there are displays of some of Mary's personal possessions.

Exit the palace through the ruins of **Holyrood Abbey,** most of which date from the late 12th and early 13th centuries. All that remains of the great abbey church is the nave; it was saved when the rest of the building was demolished in 1570 because it was being used as the Canongate Parish Church. This left the east end of the nave open. It was filled with the huge arched window you see today for Charles I's coronation in 1633. The bay on the right below the window is a royal burial vault, where lie David II, James II, James V, and Lord Darnley.

Holyrood Park, the ancient hunting ground of Scottish kings, rises beyond the palace. Its highest point (251 metres/823 feet) is the summit of Arthur's Seat, which can easily be climbed from the parking area by Dunsapie Loch on the east side. The view from the top is extraordinary—on a clear day you can see the Fife hills across the Firth of Forth, North Berwick Law, and the Bass Rock 32 km (20 miles) to the east, and even the peaks of the southern Highlands. On the hill above Holyroodhouse you'll find St. Margaret's Well, and the 15th-century ruins of **St. Anthony's Chapel.** A walk offering grand views over the Old Town follows the Radical Road, climbing from Holyrood along the foot of Salisbury Crags.

Grassmarket & Greyfriars

The deep hollow beneath the south face of the Castle Rock is filled by the Grassmarket, one of the Old Town's former marketplaces. In 1477 James III authorized the holding of markets here, with cattle being sold at the west end, and farming implements, tack and other equipment at the east. Today it is a broad, sunny street with many lively pubs— sidewalk tables line the pavement in the summer. In one of the taverns, the **White Hart Inn,** Robert Burns lodged during his final visit to Edinburgh in 1791.

But this gaiety disguises a ghoulish past— the Grassmarket was for a long time the city's main place of execution. The **Covenanters' Memorial** at the east end of the street marks the site of the gallows where over 100 Covenanters, and many others beside, met their end. At the other end of the street is the West Port, the site of one of the six gates in the city walls that were built in the aftermath of Flodden. Very little remains of the **Flodden Wall.** The main relic is up a narrow close on the left called the Vennel—at the top of the stairs you can see a battlemented tower with loopholes.

Across from the Covenanters' Memorial, a street called Candlemaker Row slopes up to meet George IV Bridge beside the statue of **Greyfriars Bobby.** The little dog's grave is just inside the entrance to Greyfriars Kirkyard (left of the pub); the grave of his master, Jock Gray, is down to the right.

Greyfriars Kirkyard has an important place in Scottish history: the National Covenant was signed here in 1638. The Martyrs' Memorial, beside the wall overlooking Candlemaker Row, remembers those who died for their convictions. Figures buried in the kirkyard include James Douglas, Earl of Morton, Regent of Scotland from 1572-1578 (c. 1516-1581); the poet Allan Ramsay (1686-1758); the architect William Adam (1689-1748); James Hutton, "Father of Modern Geology" (1726-97); and the editor of the *Encyclopaedia Britannica*, William Smellie (1740-1795).

Opposite the entrance to Greyfriars is Chambers Street, home to the **Royal Museum of Scotland** (see page 60). This impressive Victorian building, dating from 1861, has a splendid Main Hall with a glass roof and wrought-iron balconies, and houses fascinating collections covering natural history, technology, Chinese and Islamic decorative art, Asiatic sculpture, and ancient Egypt.

NEW TOWN

Between the end of the 14th century and the start of the 18th, the population of Edinburgh increased from 2,000 to 50,000.

A Faithful Friend

Greyfriars Bobby was a Skye terrier belonging to "Auld Jock" Gray, a local police constable. When Jock died in 1858, Bobby followed the funeral procession, and stayed by his master's grave. He remained for 14 years, leaving only to be fed at a nearby tavern. Impressed by such fidelity, the Lord Provost gave him a licence, as he was legally a stray and might be put down. Bobby's story so captured the local imagination, that a bronze statue of him was raised in 1873, soon after his death. His collar and bowl can be seen in Huntly House Museum.

The ever-more squalid and overcrowded conditions that afflicted the Old Town prompted the Lord Provost to suggest building an extension of the city on the ridge to the north, and in 1766 a competition was announced to find the best scheme. The winner was James Craig, a 23-year-old self-taught architect, who envisaged a symmetrical grid of streets bounded by a square at either end. The street names celebrated the Royal Family of the day— George Street for the king; Queen Street for his wife; and Princes Street for their son—as well as the recent Union of Scotland and England

Greyfriars Bobby sat 14 years at his owner's grave.

Thistle Street and Rose Street, St. Andrew Square and St. George Square (later renamed Charlotte Square).

Construction of the North Bridge began in 1763 to provide access from the Old Town across the marshy valley of the Nor' Loch, and between 1781 and 1830 some 2 million cartloads of earth taken from the New Town foundations were used to build The Mound, halfway along Princes Street. The New Town soon became popular with the wealthier citizens of Edinburgh, and was extended to the north and west, and around the slopes of Calton Hill, to form what has been described as "the most extensive example of a Romantic Classical city in the world."

Princes Street

The southern edge of the New Town is defined by Princes Street, Edinburgh's principal shopping street. Its unique character comes from being built up on one side only, affording shoppers fine views of the Castle and the Old Town. The marshy depression of the Nor'Loch was drained in the early 19th century and laid out as **Princes Street Gardens.** At the west end is St. Cuthbert's Parish Church, constructed in 1892-1895, but occupying a site of great antiquity — the original St. Cuthbert's was at least 12th-century, and may date back to the seventh century.

In the middle of the western gardens you'll find the **Ross Bandstand,** a setting for open-air concerts during the summer, including the Fireworks Concert on the last Thursday of the Festival. At the steps up to The Mound you can see the skill of the gardeners who create the famous **Floral Clock,** which dates from 1903. The Mound itself is dominated by the Doric temple of the **Royal Scottish Academy** (see page 60), and the Ionic porticoes of the **National Gallery of Scotland** (see page 60), both designed by William Henry Playfair.

The National Gallery's collection (European artists from 1300-1900) is one of the best of its size in the world; not surprisingly, the collection of Scottish paintings is particularly fine. Highlights include the *Madonna and Child* by Andrea del Verrocchio, *Three Ages of Man* by Raphael, *Old Woman Cooking Eggs* by Velazquez, the *Trinity Altarpiece* by Hugo van der Goes, *The Seven Sacraments* by Poussin, and *Vision of the Sermon* by Gauguin. Scottish favourites include *The Artist's Wife* by Allan Ramsay (the poet's son), *The Reverend Robert Walker Skating on Duddingston Loch* by Henry Raeburn, and *Pitlessie Fair* by David Wilkie. Another crowd-pleaser is the Vaughan bequest of Turner water-colours, which are exhibited once a year in January. (The gallery was built over the railway tunnel on the approach to Waverley, and as you admire the paintings you will occasionally notice the deep rumbling of a passing train.)

Princes Street's most distinctive landmark is the soaring Gothic spire of the **Scott Monument.** It was constructed in 1840–1844 to the design of George Meikle Kemp, a previously unknown draughtsman, to commemorate the great Edinburgh novelist Sir Walter Scott, who died in 1832. Inspired by the Gothic architecture of Melrose Abbey, it includes 64 statuettes of characters from Scott's novels. The statue at the foot of the monument shows Scott with his deerhound Maida; this was carved from a 30-ton block of Italian marble by John Steell in 1840-1846. A climb of 287 steps leads to the upper gallery where you can enjoy an excellent view of the city centre. Currently closed for repairs, it is expected to reopen in 1999.

Calton Hill

The east end of Princes Street is overlooked by the black crags of Calton Hill, formed by lava flows erupted from the ancient volcano of Arthur's Seat. The summit of the hill is graced with a variety of monuments, most notably the slender, 30-metre (98-foot) tower of the **Nelson Monument,**

Princes Street Gardens is a popular spot for sunbathers and postcard-writers.

raised in 1807–1815 in memory of Admiral Nelson's victory at Trafalgar. You can climb to the top (fee), where a crosstree supports a ball that was dropped daily at 1:00 P.M. as a time-signal for ships in the Firth of Forth.

The **National Monument,** on the very summit, was intended to be a copy of the Parthenon in Athens, and a memorial for those who died during the Napoleonic Wars. It was begun in 1826, but work stopped after three years when the money ran out, with just the western end finished. The **City Observatory** was built in 1818 for the purpose of measuring time through astronomical observation (important for navigation in the days before satellites). Smoke from Waverley Station forced the astronomers to move in 1895, and the building now houses the "Edinburgh Experience," a 3-D slide show celebrating the city. It is open from April to October daily 10:00 A.M.-5:00 P.M.

The colonnade below the observatory is a memorial to Dugald Stewart (1753-1828), Professor of Moral Philosophy at Edinburgh University. The structure beside Regent Road on the south flank of the hill is the Burns Monument (1830).

George Street

George Street, not Princes Street, was the main thoroughfare in Craig's 1766 plan for the New Town. It was the principal axis of the regular grid, running along the crest of the ridge between the two great squares. The oldest surviving houses in the New Town were built on **St. Andrew Square,** the finest of which is the Royal Bank of Scotland headquarters on the east side. Downhill from the bus station, on the corner of Queen Street, you'll find the **Scottish National Portrait Gallery** (see page 60).

A little way along George Street, on the right, is the **Church of St. Andrew and St. George,** built in 1782–1784 with an unusual oval floor-plan. It was the setting for the Disruption of 1843, when 474 ministers walked out of the General Assembly to form the Free Church, one of many schisms which divided the Church of Scotland in the course of its long history. Between George Street and Princes Street lies **Rose Street,** originally intended to house the New Town's humbler inhabitants, but now a pedestrianized shopping precinct, famous for its pubs. Its northern counterpart, **Thistle Street,** is quieter, lined with antique shops and bistros.

The undoubted masterpiece of the New Town is **Charlotte Square,** built in 1792–1805 to the design of Robert Adam. The elegant façade along the north side is generally thought to be one of the world's finest examples of Georgian architecture. In the centre is Bute House, the office of the Secretary of State for Scotland; next door is the **Georgian House,** restored in period style by the National Trust for Scotland. The westward vista along George Street is dominated by the dome of **West Register House,** on the west side of the square. It was originally St. George's Church but was taken over by the government in 1960 and is now used for storage of public records.

An inscription at 16 South Charlotte Street records that Alexander Graham Bell, the inventor of the telephone, was born there on 3 March 1847. Another of Edinburgh's most famous sons was also a New Town resident: Robert Louis Stevenson lived at 17 Heriot Row during 1857–1880. A plaque beneath the gas lamp by the door (now electric) has a verse of *Leerie the Lamplighter,* inspired by childhood memories of seeing the lamps being lit:

For we are very lucky with a lamp before the door,
And Leerie stops to light it as he lights so many more,
And O! before you hurry by with ladder and with light,
O Leerie, see a little child and nod to him tonight.

The Georgian terraces of the New Town provide elegant accommodation.

EDINBURGH'S VILLAGES

As the city of Edinburgh expanded in the 20th century, it absorbed many of the small villages around it. These ancient communities, with their parish churches, historic buildings, and strong local traditions, still manage to maintain a distinctive identity within the city's boundaries.

Leith

Leith, about 3 km (2 miles) northeast of the city centre, has been the port of Edinburgh since the 14th century, and until as recently as 1920 was still a completely independent burgh with its own town council. Dependent on the docks, the town's fortunes declined in the aftermath of World War II, but in the past few years the area has been revived. Old buildings have been restored as offices and flats; new pubs, restaurants, and hotels have opened; and the old waterfront is now a vibrant and attractive lunch and dinner spot.

The heart of the old town is clustered around the quays at the mouth of the **Water of Leith,** a little river that winds a leafy course through the centre of Edinburgh. A walkway has been built alongside the river bank for much of its length, and should eventually allow walkers to follow the stream all the way from Leith to the village of Balerno, 22 km (14 miles) away on the edge of the Pentland Hills.

The most attractive part of Leith is **The Shore,** where Commercial Street crosses the river beside the 19th-century Customs House. The old quayside and cobbled lanes have been renovated, and there are many attractive bars and restaurants, including one on a ship moored in the stream. A plaque at No. 30 The Shore, marks the **King's Landing,** the spot where King George IV stepped ashore on his visit to Edinburgh in 1822. North of the bridge, on the right bank, is the circular **Signal Tower,** constructed in 1686, and originally a windmill for making rapeseed oil. Beyond it is the 19th-century Sailors' Home, now restored as a fashionable hotel and brasserie.

Across the bridge is Commercial Street, bordered by 19th-century warehouses; in contrast, the names of Cromwell Street and Citadel Street on the left recall the 1650s, when Cromwell's army occupied Edinburgh and built a fort in Leith to control the harbour. Back inland is the park called **Leith Links,** famed as "The Home of Golf," where the Honourable Company of Edinburgh Golfers erected their clubhouse in 1767. A plaque mounted on a stone cairn on the west side tells how the game was played here during the 18th century. There was a five-hole course, with each hole measuring more than 400 yards. A list of 13 rules was drawn up for a tournament held on Leith Links in 1744, and these formed the basis of the modern game of golf.

Immediately to the west of Leith is the former fishing village of **Newhaven,** with its harbour nestled into the western breakwater of the docks. Newhaven was founded by James IV in the 16th century as a naval dockyard, and it was here that the *Great Michael* (see page 19) was constructed and launched. In the 18th and 19th centuries the village was famous for its fishwives, who supplied the city

Museums and Art Galleries

Huntly House Museum: 142 Canongate. A fascinating museum of local history, recording the growth of Edinburgh. Open 10:00 A.M.-5:30 P.M. Monday-Saturday (during the Edinburgh Festival, Sundays 2:00-5:00 P.M.). Free.

Museum of Childhood: 42 High Street. Displays relating to the health, education and upbringing of children in times past. Open 10:00 A.M.-5:30 P.M. Monday-Saturday (during the Edinburgh Festival, Sundays 2:00-5:00 P.M.). Free.

National Gallery of Scotland: The Mound. One of the best small collections in Europe, with works spanning from the 14th-20th centuries. Especially fine collection of Scottish works. Open 10:00 A.M.-5:00 P.M. Monday-Saturday, 2:00-5:00 P.M. Sunday. Free.

People's Story Museum: Canongate Tolbooth. A museum of social history, recording the life and work of Edinburgh's ordinary folk from the late 18th century to the present. Open 10:00 A.M.-5:30 P.M. Monday to Saturday (during the Edinburgh Festival, Sundays 2:00-5:00 P.M.). Free.

Royal Museum of Scotland: Chambers Street. Superb Victorian building, housing collections relating to natural history, geology, science, technology, decorative arts, and more. Open 10:00 A.M.-5:00 P.M. (from 12 noon on Sunday). Free.

Royal Scottish Academy: The Mound. Work by Academy members, plus a special exhibition during the Festival. Open 10:00 A.M.-5:00 P.M. Monday-Saturday, 2:00-5:00 P.M Sunday. Admission fee is dependent upon the particular exhibition.

Scottish National Gallery of Modern Art: Belford Road. The country's top collection of 20th-century art, including several works by Picasso, Matisse, and Henry Moore. Open 10:00 A.M.-5:00 P.M. Monday-Saturday, 2:00 A.M.-5:00 P.M. Sunday. Free.

Scottish National Portrait Gallery & Museum of Antiquities: 1 Queen Street. Portraits of prominent figures from Scottish history, and an exhibition covering Scotland throughout the ages. Open 10:00 A.M.-5:00 P.M. Monday-Saturday, 2:00 A.M.-5:00 P.M. Sunday. Free.

Writers' Museum: Lady Stair's Close, Lawnmarket. Memorabilia relating to Robert Burns, Sir Walter Scott, and R. L. Stevenson. Open 10:00 A.M.-5:30 P.M. Monday-Saturday (during the Edinburgh Festival, Sundays 2:00-5:00 P.M.). Free.

gentry with fresh oysters and herring. Victoria School in the Main Street houses the local **museum.**

Cramond

Cramond, with its rivermouth setting, whitewashed houses, and resident swans, is one of Edinburgh's prettiest villages. It takes its name from the **fort** that was built at the mouth of the River Almond by the Romans in the second century A.D. (*Caer Almond* means the "Fort on the Almond"). The fort was the eastern end of a line of defences that became the Antonine Wall. The foundations of the Roman buildings are on view in the grounds around the church; objects found during the archaeological excavations are displayed in Huntly House Museum (see opposite page).

More modern fortifications are evident in the form of a line of tapered concrete pillars, which runs from the rivermouth to **Cramond Island** about a mile offshore. This is a World War II anti-submarine barrier, built as part of the defences of Rosyth Naval Base, which lies upstream from the Forth Bridges. Old gun emplacements can be seen on the island, which is accessible at low tide. (**Note:** Check **tide times** carefully before walking out to the island. Every year dozens of people are trapped by the incoming tide and have to be rescued by the lifeboat.)

Cramond Kirk was built in 1656 (much altered since),

Many of Leith's new establishments honour the town's nautical heritage.

but the church tower is even older, dating from the 15th century. On the far side of the church you'll find **Cramond Tower,** a 15th-century tower house that once belonged to the Bishops of Dunkeld. It has been restored and is now used as a private residence.

During the 18th century the **water mills** along the River Almond, which had ground the corn from the surrounding farms for hundreds of years, were caught up in the industrial revolution and converted to iron mills. Between 1750 and 1810, the Cramond ironworks turned out thousands of tons of iron nails, barrel hoops, hoes, spades, chains, and anchors. The ruined mill buildings and their neighbouring weirs are a feature of the pleasant riverside walk up to the Cramond Bridge Hotel.

Back at the quay, the Cramond ferryman will row you across the river, between the moored yachts, to the grounds of the Rosebery estate on the far bank. From here

a fine walk leads along the shore past the **Eagle Rock** (a natural outcrop with an ancient carved eagle) to **Dalmeny House,** the seat of the Earls of Rosebery. This stately home is open to the public from May to September, and contains a fine collection of tapestries, furniture, and porcelain, and paintings by Gainsborough, Reynolds, Raeburn, and Mil-

A 15th-century church tower watches over the lovely town of Cramond.

lais. The fifth earl was a great admirer of Napoleon Bona-
parte, and the Napoleon Room holds many interesting
relics of the Emperor. You can walk along the shore all the
way to Queensferry, 7 km (4 miles) from Cramond, where
buses and trains head back to the city centre.

Dean Village

If you walk down Queensferry Street from the west end of
Princes Street, you soon arrive at the deep valley of the Water
of Leith, which is spanned by the lofty arches of the **Dean
Bridge,** built in 1829–1832 by Thomas Telford, one of Scotland's greatest civil engineers (also responsible for the Caledonian Canal, and the Menai Bridge in Wales). In the years
following its completion, the 105-foot- (32 metre-) high bridge
became such a popular site for suicides that in 1912 the parapets were raised and topped with iron spikes as a deterrent.

Unfortunately these raised parapets also prevent shorter
passersby from enjoying the fine view down to the attractive
Dean Village, which nestles in the valley below. Before the
Dean Bridge was built, all traffic (horse-drawn of course) travelling from Edinburgh to Queensferry had to descend the steep
hill of **Bell's Brae,** cross the old village bridge, then climb la-
boriously up the far side. Like Cramond, Dean was a mill village, and its history is inextricably linked with the
"Incorporation of Baxters," the bakers' guild. At the old bridge,
take a look at the parapet on the right, where you will see a
stone carved with crossed "peels" (bakers' shovels for putting
loaves into the oven) and the words "Blesit be god for al his
giftis." On the door lintel of the house behind you is another
carving showing crossed peels with three loaves, and the words
"God bless the Baxters of Edinburgh uho bult this hous 1675"
[sic]. The huge building on the other side of the bridge is the
West Mill, built in 1805, but now converted to private flats.

The Water of Leith once powered the flour mills of picturesque Dean Village.

Don't cross the bridge, but go left up the narrow cobbled alley of Hawthornbank Lane, under the half-timbered façade of Hawthorn Buildings (1895). Then cross the river at the footbridge, which occupies the site of the ancient ford (you can see the old road stones in the water), and follow the walkway by the riverbank. A walk of about 15 minutes takes you under Belford Bridge, and past the Hilton Hotel, where you recross the stream. At the next footbridge a sign directs you up a path on the far bank to reach the **Scottish National Gallery of Modern Art.** The Neoclassical building, set in marvellous grounds, was formerly a school, but nowadays houses an outstanding collection of 20th-century art. It has masterpieces by Picasso, Matisse, Miro, Giacometti, and Henry Moore, and works by Scottish artists such as Peploe, Fergusson, Hunter, and Cadell. There is an attractive garden-café downstairs.

 Duddingston

The tiny village of Duddingston enjoys a surprisingly rural setting, squeezed between the southeastern flank of Arthur's Seat and the reedy waters of Duddingston Loch. On the wooded promontory overlooking the loch is **Dud-**

dingston Kirk, one of the oldest Scottish churches still in
regular use. It was founded by the monks of Kelso in the
12th century, and still retains the basic form of the original
Norman church, with a tower and north transept added in
the 17th century. The old Norman doorway in the south
wall (now blocked) has an arch decorated with chevrons,
and on the left-hand shaft a carving of Christ on the cross.
At the kirkyard gate is an octagonal tower, constructed in
1824 as a **watchtower** to deter body snatchers from steal-
ing newly buried corpses (money was to be made by selling
bodies to anatomy professors). Close to hand is the
Loupin-on Stane, a 17th-century device to help parish-
ioners get up on to their horses after Sunday service, and
the **Joug Collar,** a device for punishing all who strayed
from the straight and narrow.

The village proper lies just across the road from the church,
along the street called The Causeway. On the corner is the old
Sheep Heid Inn, a fine 18th-century tavern with a skittle alley
at the back. The name comes from the traditional dish of *pow-
sowdie*—a broth or stew made by boiling up a sheep's head—
which was once served regularly in the inn. Also on The
Causeway, identified by an engraving in the stone, is **Prince
Charlie's Cottage.** The Young Pretender stayed here during
his brief occupation of Edinburgh in 1745 before marching east
to defeat Sir John Cope's army at the Battle of Prestonpans.

The wooded southern shore of Duddingston Loch is a nature reserve, and the loch itself has been a bird sanctuary
since 1925. Amateur ornithologists use a special hide to study
the flocks of waterfowl that gather here, especially in winter.

Swanston

The picture-postcard village of Swanston lies snuggled in a
fold of the Pentland Hills on the southernmost fringe of the

city. Its cluster of thatched, whitewashed cottages is set around a village green that marks the start of many a walk in the hills. At the top of the green is a bench with a plaque dedicated to the poet Edwin Muir (1887–1959) who came here "to linger and meditate."

But the name that will be forever associated with Swanston is that of **Robert Louis Stevenson,** whose father took over the lease on the nearby house called Swanston Cottage in 1867. For the next 13 years the Stevenson family used the house as a weekend retreat and holiday home, hoping that the country air would prove beneficial to their sickly son. The young writer fell in love with the Pentland Hills, with their rich past and spreading views of the city, and many years later, thousands of miles away in Samoa (where he died at the age of 44), he remembered them with deep emotion:

Be it granted to me to behold you again in dying,
Hills of home! and to hear again the call;
Hear about the graves of the martyrs the peewees crying,
And hear no more at all.

OUTLYING AREAS

A number of Edinburgh's visitor attractions lie around the edges of the city; most are accessible by bus (see page 124).

Blackford Hill

The craggy slopes of Blackford Hill, rising to a height of 164 metres (538 feet), provide one of the best viewpoints in the city. From this vantage point, about 3 km (2 miles) south of Princes Street, you can look across the Victorian suburbs of Grange and Marchmont to the long jagged spine of the Old Town, stretching between the Castle Rock and the tilted cliffs of Salisbury Crags. In the other direction lie the green slopes of the Braid Hills, with the heathered Pentlands beyond.

Blackford Hill was bought for the city in 1884 by Lord Provost Sir George Harrison, who is commemorated by a red sandstone archway at the bottom of Observatory Road, which leads up the hill. At the top is the **Royal Observatory,** which was built in the 1890s to replace the outdated City Observatory on Calton Hill (see page 56), and which played an important part in the growth of astronomy in Scotland. The Observatory today houses a Visitor Centre with exhibitions on astronomy and the history of the Blackford Hill site. Open year-round Monday-Saturday 10:00 A.M.-5:00 P.M. and Sunday noon-5:00 P.M.; closed December 22-January 3.

On the south side of Blackford Hill lies the lovely wooded glen called the **Hermitage of Braid,** with a Countryside Information Centre at its west end. A nature trail follows the little stream winding through the trees, and there are other walks to be explored.

Craigmillar Castle

On the southeastern edge of Edinburgh lies one of Scotland's best-preserved medieval castles. Craigmillar Castle was built by the Preston family, who were the lairds of Craigmillar from the 14th century until 1660. Sir William Preston (laird 1442–1453) presented the High Kirk with a relic of St. Giles (a bone from his arm), and is remembered in the Preston Aisle of St. Giles' Cathedral. His great-great-grandson, Sir Simon Preston, was one of Mary Queen of Scots' most loyal supporters, and as a result the queen stayed at Craigmillar on several occasions, notably during the aftermath of Rizzio's murder and the birth of James VI. The castle was sold to Sir John Gilmour, a lawyer, and later lord president of the Court of Session, in 1660. The Gilmours held the place until they moved on to

Inch House in nearby Gilmerton in the 1770s, after which the castle fell into disrepair.

Despite two centuries of neglect, the ruins of Craigmillar Castle are well worth seeing. The early 15th-century tower house still stands to its full height, and is surrounded by a variety of later 15th- and 16th-century curtain walls, turrets, and ranges, in an attractive rural setting to the south of Arthur's Seat. Open between April and September Monday to Saturday 9:30 A.M.-6:30 P.M., Sunday 2:00-6:30 P.M.; October to March from Monday to Thursday 9:30 A.M.-4:30 P.M. (though closed Thursday afternoons), Sunday 2:00-4:30 P.M.

Edinburgh Zoo

Edinburgh's famous zoo was founded by the Royal Zoological Society of Scotland in 1913 and nowadays spreads for over 32½ hectares (80 acres) across the southern slopes of Corstorphine Hill. The zoo is involved in a long-term conservation programme, and looks after endangered species such as the red panda, the snow leopard, the pygmy hippo, the white rhino, the lowland gorilla, and the Siberian tiger. But it is best-known to visitors for its famous penguin colony, which has over 150 birds from three different species—king penguins, gentoos, and macaronis. The huge enclosure includes an underwater viewing window. Each day at 2:00 P.M. (March to October only) the ever-popular Penguin Parade takes place, when the birds go for a promenade outside their enclosure.

Lauriston Castle

The site of Lauriston Castle, in the northwestern corner of the city, commands a breathtaking panorama of the Firth of Forth, over Cramond Island, Inchmickery, and Inchcolm to the coast of Fife and the Lomond Hills. The nucleus of the castle is a tower house, built in the 1590s by Sir

Archibald Napier, whose son John Napier of Merchiston was the famous mathematician and inventor of logarithms. But the castle was greatly extended in the 19th century, and now stands as a fine example of an elegant Edwardian country house. Its last private owner, the Edinburgh businessman William Reid, bought the castle in 1902 to house his collection of period furniture and art, and in 1926 bequeathed both house and contents to the nation. Open between April and October Monday-Thursday 11:00 A.M.-5:00 P.M. (closed 1:00-2:00 P.M. except mid-June to mid-September); from November to March weekends only, 2:00-4:00 P.M. Grounds open all year 9:00 A.M.-dusk.

Queensferry

Queensferry, a village 13 km (8 miles) west of Edinburgh, owes its name to Queen Margaret, wife of the Scottish king Malcolm Canmore (1057–1093), whose ferry used to cross the Firth of Forth here on her travels between Edinburgh and Dunfermline Palace (see page 77). By the shore at the west end of the village, a memorial plaque marks the site of **The Binks,** a natural jetty formed by a rocky outcrop, where the ferry boat used to come ashore.

The Queen's Ferry has long since been rendered obsolete by the two enormous bridges which span the Forth on either side of the vilage. The **Forth Railway Bridge** was completed in 1890, and was one of the greatest feats of Victorian engineering. The three huge cantilevers, each 411 metres (1,350 feet) long, are joined by two suspended spans of 107 metres (350 feet) each, making a total length of 1,447 metres (4,746 feet) between the end piers—for many years this counted as the longest bridge in the world. Its construction required no less than 59,000 tonnes of steel. The story of the bridge, and the history of Queensferry, are recorded inside the Queensfer-

*The harbour at Queensferry is overlooked by the graceful
spans of the Forth Railway Bridge.*

ry Museum in the village High Street. The museum is open
mid-January through December on Monday and Thursday-
Saturday 10:00 A.M.-5:00 P.M., on Sunday noon-5:00 P.M.

Ferries continued to ply the waters of the Forth until 1964,
when the **Forth Road Bridge** was opened. This fine suspension bridge links Lothian to Fife with a single unsupported
span of 1,006 metres (3,300 feet)—for two years it was the
longest suspension bridge in Europe, until Lisbon's Ponte
Salazar pipped it by 7 metres (23 feet). Even today, it is ex-
ceeded in length in Europe only by England's Humber
Bridge (1981) and the two Bosphorus bridges in Istanbul
(1973 and 1988). At the north end of the bridge you'll find
Deep Sea World, a major aquarium with viewing tunnels allowing you to observe sharks at close range (see page 31).

The jetty below the Railway Bridge is the departure point for boat trips to **Inchcolm,** an island in the Firth of Forth (from Easter to October only). Inchcolm is often called the "Iona of the East," as it is the home of the ruined medieval Abbey of St. Colm, founded by Alexander I in the 12th century. (St. Colm may be identified with St. Columba of Iona, who brought Christianity to western Scotland during the sixth century.) The abbey buildings are well-preserved, and offer a fascinating view of the life of a medieval monastery. Inchcolm can also be reached from Aberdour in Fife (see page 77).

Roslin Chapel

The village of Roslin, or Rosslyn, a few miles to the south of Edinburgh, is where you will find one of Britain's great masterpieces of Gothic stonework, Roslin Chapel, built in the 15th century for Sir William St. Clair, the Third Earl of Orkney. It was originally intended to be a much larger church, but only the choir was completed before Sir William's death, after which the project ground to a halt. The interior of the chapel is a virtuoso display of the mason's art, with elaborately carved columns and capitals decorated with flowers, and bas-reliefs showing the Cardinal Virtues, the Seven Deadly Sins, and the Dance of Death.

At the eastern end of the chapel, close by the stairway to the crypt, is the **Apprentice Pillar.** According to local legend, an apprentice created this beautiful pillar while the master mason was away. When the latter returned and saw the pillar, he murdered the apprentice in a fit of jealousy. On the wall at the other end of the church are three stone heads, which are supposed to be the unfortunate apprentice (the one on the left, with a wound on its head), his grieving mother, and the master mason. The chapel is open Easter to October 10:00 A.M.-5:00 P.M. (from noon on Sunday).

Royal Botanic Garden

The long history of the city's Botanic Garden stretches back for more than 300 years, making it the second oldest in Britain after Oxford's. Edinburgh's original "Physic Garden" was founded in 1670 not far from Holyrood Abbey, and between 1675 and 1763 it occupied a site at the east end of Waverley Station. Its creators were Sir Robert Sibbald, the first Professor of Medicine at Edinburgh University, as well as Physician to His Majesty Charles II; and Sir Andrew Balfour, a noted physician and botanist. They were primarily interested in the medicinal effects of the various plants that they cultivated. After a spell on a site near Leith Walk, the Botanic Garden was eventually moved to its present location in Inverleith, a mile north of Princes Street, in 1823.

The modern gardens cover 28 hectares (70 acres) on a low hill to the north of the city centre, with splendid views of the castle, Old Town, Calton Hill, and Salisbury Crags. The beautifully landscaped grounds include a colossal glasshouse complex housing tropical and temperate palms, ferns, cycads and orchids, woodland, rock and heath gardens, and the biggest and most spectacular collection of rhododendrons in Britain. Open daily from 9:30 A.M. (in March through September until 6:00 P.M.; February and October until 5:00 P.M.; and November through January until 4:00 P.M.).

EXCURSIONS

There are plenty of interesting places for a day trip from Edinburgh. Most can be reached by bus or train (see page 124).

East to Dunbar

The coastal plain to the east of Edinburgh was once the main invasion route between Scotland and England, and retains a rich legacy of castles, battle-field sites, and historical associations. **Prestonpans,** owing its name to the salt pans that once provided its livelihood, is remembered for the Battle of Prestonpans (1745), when forces led by Prince Charles Edward Stuart (Bonnie Prince Charlie) defeated an English army under General Sir John Cope. The battlefield site is east of the town, inland from the prominent chim-

Huge tropical palms grow in the Botanic Garden.

neys of Cockenzie Power Station. A more recent past is on show in the **Scottish Mining Museum** at nearby Newtongrange, with records of the district's coal-mining heritage. Open March–October daily 10:00 A.M.–4:00 P.M.

West of the beaches and golf links of Gullane stretches the nature reserve of **Aberlady Bay,** a haven for the flocks of wildfowl that gather to feed on its tidal mudflats, and a magnet for ornithologists from all over the country. East of Gullane lies the pretty village of **Dirleton** with its fine, ruined castle. A conspicuous feature of the landscape is **Berwick Law,** a conical hill capped by an arch made from a whale's jawbone. The view from the summit is impressive—during the Napoleonic Wars the hill served as a lookout against invasion by the French fleet.

Between Berwick Law and the sea lies the attractive Victorian seaside resort of **North Berwick,** with a good sandy beach, two golf courses, and inviting tearooms. Boat trips from the harbour will take you to see the **Bass Rock,** a towering, cliff-girt islet a few miles offshore. The rock was once the site of a castle, and was used in the 17th century as a prison for Covenanters; today it is the home of thousands of seabirds, and one of Britain's biggest gannet colonies. A few miles east you will find the spectacular ruins of **Tantallon Castle.** A great curtain wall of red sandstone sits astride an isthmus, defending the approach to a narrow headland which is protected on the other three sides by sheer sea cliffs. The castle dates for the most part from the 14th century, and provided a stronghold for the powerful earls of Douglas. Its great strength was proved by the fact that it was not captured until 1651, when Cromwell sent General Monk, accompanied by a great artillery train, to besiege the castle. After 12 days of heavy bombardment a breach was opened in the walls and Tantallon was taken, but the castle was so badly damaged that it had to be abandoned. Open from April to September daily 9:30 A.M.-6:30 P.M.; from October to March 9:30 A.M.-4:30 P.M. (closed Thursday afternoon and Friday; open from 2:00 P.M. Sunday).

The waters of the River Tyne, which flows into the sea west of Dunbar, have powered the wheels of **Preston Mill** for 350 years. This 17th-century water mill is still in working order, and was even being used commercially until the 1950s. Now owned by the National Trust for Scotland, it is open to the public as a working museum, offering a good insight into 17th-century rural life.

The royal burgh of **Dunbar** lies 37 km (23 miles) east of Edinburgh, clustered around a ruined castle and picturesque harbour. Nearby, on the banks of the Spott Burn, the forces of Edward I routed the Scots in 1296; and in 1650 Cromwell's army inflicted a humiliating defeat on the Scottish supporters of Charles II. The castle, which once stood on the headland above the harbour, was one of the places where Mary Queen of Scots sought refuge following the murder of Rizzio (see page 49). It was destroyed by her enemy, the Earl of Moray, and all that remain are a few crumbling fragments of wall.

In the town's High Street is **John Muir House,** the birthplace of the man who helped create the American national parks system. John Muir was born in Dunbar in 1838 and emigrated to the U.S. together with his family at the age of 11. He became a naturalist and an influential writer campaigning for the preservation of California's wild forests and mountains, and eventually helped create Yosemite National Park in 1890. The house honours his life and work. Some scenic coastline to the west of Dunbar has been designated the **John Muir Country Park,** and offers several attractive walks

West to Stirling

A few miles west of Queensferry is **Hopetoun House,** perhaps the most splendid stately home in Scotland. Built during the first half of the 18th century to the designs of William Adam and his son John, the house is the seat of the Marquis of Linlithgow. It contains magnificent apartments, paintings by Titian, Rubens, and Gainsborough, and priceless collections of china, tapestries, and period costume. The quiet, lovely wooded grounds, overlooking the Firth of Forth, contain herds of deer and a flock of the rare four-horned St. Kilda sheep. Open April-September daily 10:00 A.M.-5:30 P.M.

The Royal and Ancient Burgh of **Linlithgow** enjoys an attractive setting on the southern shore of a small loch, beside the massive walls of the fortified palace where James V was born in 1512, and his daughter Mary Queen of Scots was born in 1542. The promontory had been occupied by a royal manor house for 300 years when work on the present palace began in 1425. Building continued for over a century, resulting in a huge, square structure ranged around a central courtyard. Following the Union of the

Crowns in 1603 the palace fell into neglect, and in 1746 the building was gutted by fire. The ruins are still impressive. Adjacent to the palace is the **Parish Church of St. Michael,** its tower crowned by a modern aluminum spire. The church is famed for its fine Gothic window tracery, and the ghost who foretold James IV of his defeat at Flodden. Open April to September 9:30 A.M.-6:30 P.M. (from 2:00 P.M. Sunday); between October and March 9:30 A.M.-4:30 P.M. (from 2:00 P.M. Sunday).

The region between Edinburgh and Stirling has been called "Scotland's Battlefield," because of the many clashes between English and Scottish forces that took place here. A famous Scottish victory was won by Robert the Bruce at **Bannockburn** in 1314, when he routed Edward II's army and assured Scotland's independence (for a time, at least). The exact location of the battlefield is disputed, though it was somewhere on the banks of the Bannock Burn, which lies a few miles south of Stirling. The National Trust for Scotland maintains a **Heritage Centre** at the most likely site, with an exhibition describing the background to the battle. Nearby an equestrian statue of Robert the Bruce surveys the scene of his greatest triumph.

Edward II's main objective in 1314 was **Stirling Castle,** one of Scotland's great royal strongholds. This guarded the strategically important bridge over the River Forth, and was for centuries equal in status to Edinburgh Castle, with which it has many similarities. Much of the castle dates from the 16th century, particularly the reign of James V (1513–1542), who constructed the imposing Royal Palace. The infant Mary Queen of Scots was crowned in the Chapel Royal here in 1543, and her son James VI was crowned nearby in the Church of the Holy Rude. The Castle is open daily 9:30 A.M.-6:00 P.M. (5:00 P.M. October-March).

Another important Scottish victory was won nearby in 1297, when William Wallace repulsed the English invaders at the Battle of Stirling Bridge. The **Auld Brig** over the Forth is certainly old, but not of Wallace's day—dating rather from the late 15th or early 16th century. The arch at the west end was rebuilt in 1749, having been blown up to stop Bonnie Prince Charlie's Highlanders entering the town in 1745. The hilltop tower on the far side of the river is the 19th-century **Wallace Monument,** housing Wallace's two-handed sword.

North to Fife

Across the Forth lies the ancient Pictish kingdom of Fife, one of Scotland's most fertile regions. Its farmland brought wealth to the earls who held it, and its forests were a favourite hunting ground of kings. During the 11th century, Malcolm Canmore and Queen Margaret constructed their royal palace at **Dunfermline,** and soon afterwards founded an Augustinian priory nearby. Although later overtaken in importance by the castles of Edinburgh and Stirling, Dunfermline remained a favourite royal retreat—it was rebuilt by James IV in 1500, and both the children of James VI (Charles I and his sister Elizabeth) were born there. Today, only a few crumbling walls of the palace remain, but the abbey church across the road preserves a wonderful Romanesque nave, built in the 12th century on the site of Queen Margaret's original chapel; Malcolm and Margaret were buried nearby. The 13th-century choir was destroyed during the Reformation, but was replaced with the present Gothic building in the 19th century, and it now serves as the parish church. It contains the grave of Robert the Bruce, who died in 1329. His heart, however, lies elsewhere—it was removed by his friend, Sir James Douglas, who carried it on a Crusade to the Holy Land, intending to bury it in Jerusalem. Sadly, he died in battle with the Moors in Spain.

You can take a holiday from history on the Silver Sands of **Aberdour,** 10 km (23 miles) east of Dunfermline. This fine, sandy beach is backed by a wooded park, and a jetty at one end offers boat trips to Inchcolm Island (see page 71). You can't escape the past totally—Aberdour has a castle with a pleasant garden containing a circular *doocot* (Scottish for "dovecote"—pigeon pie was a popular dish in those days).

To the north of the Lomond Hills is yet another royal residence. **Falkland Palace** (16th century) was a royal hunting lodge, and a popular resort for the court of James V. James loved the place, and lavished much attention on it, gracing it with fine decoration. It was here that he died, soon after hearing the news that his sole heir would be a girl (see page 20). The guided tour of the palace will show you the ruined royal apartments, the dungeon, and the "real tennis" court, which dates from 1539. Open from April to October 11:00 A.M.-5:30 P.M., Sunday 1:30-5:30 P.M.

While Edinburgh was growing into the political capital of Scotland, the country's ecclesiastical capital was firmly entrenched at St. Andrews. At the eastern end of the town rise the ruined walls of **St. Andrews Cathedral,** the largest in Scotland—its archbishop was the most powerful churchman in the country until the abolition of episcopal rule. The cathedral was founded in 1160, but fell into ruin during the 17th century. You can enjoy a view of the ruins and the town from the top of nearby **St. Rule's Tower,** a remnant of the early 12th-century church that preceded the cathedral.

You can also see **St. Andrews Castle,** occupying a cliff-top site on the shore nearby. The castle was the seat of the Archbishops of St. Andrews, and witnessed many a death during the civil wars of the 16th century. Protestant martyrs were burned at the stake, or cast into the notorious bottle dungeon in the Sea Tower. But the Reformers had their revenge when they broke into the castle and murdered their tormentor, Cardinal Beaton, then hung his body from the parapet. One of the most fascinating parts of the castle is the tunnel that was excavated during the long siege which followed the Cardinal's murder. The attackers tried to enter the castle by digging a mine through the rock beneath the walls, but were frustrated by defenders who dug a counter mine and cut them off. Open April-September 9:30 A.M.-6:30 P.M (from 2:00 P.M. Sunday); October-March 9:30 A.M. 4:30 P.M. (from 2:00 P.M. Sunday).

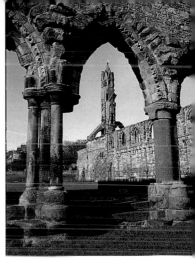

The remains of St. Andrews Cathedral recall its role as Scotland's religious capital.

No mention of St. Andrews would be complete without a word about **golf**. The town is hallowed as the home of the Royal and Ancient Golf Club, the game's ruling body, founded in 1754. There are four courses on the links to the west of town—the Jubilee, the Eden, the New, and the world-famous Old Course. You don't have to be a member to play here, but you'd be well advised to book as far in advance as you possibly can. Contact the Royal and Ancient Golf Club, St. Andrews, tel. (01334) 472 112; Reservations Office, tel. (01334) 475 757. If you can't manage a round on the links, treat yourself to a tour of the British Golf Museum, opposite the starter's box.

If you have your own transport, don't miss the chance to explore the **East Neuk,** the rugged coastline stretching between

Fife Ness and Largo Bay to the south of St. Andrews. The shore is lined with fishing harbours, ringed by houses with red pantile roofs and crow-stepped gables. **Crail** has a museum, and a 12th-century Church of St. Mary—with eighth-century Pictish sculptured stone. The larger harbour at **Anstruther** (pronounced "Enster" locally) contains a 19th-century fishing boat, *Reaper*, belonging to a marvellous Scottish Fisheries Museum on dry land—open from April to October daily 10:00 A.M.-5:30 P.M. (Sunday 11:00 A.M.-5:00 P.M.) and from November to March 10:00 A.M.-4:30 P.M. (Sunday 2:00-4:30 P.M.). From the harbour, boats go to the **Isle of May,** once a retreat for hermits, now a sanctuary for seals and birds.

One mile southwest of Anstruther is **Pittenweem,** with Flemish architecture, a daily fish market, and a cave that was once the home of St. Fillan. A path along the cliff-top leads west from the 14th-century church, **St. Monans,** to the ruins of Newark Castle. A long, sandy beach stretches between Elie

The fishing villages of Fife offer a picturesque detour along the road to St. Andrews.

and Earlsferry, and continues beyond the headland around Largo Bay, a playground for local windsurfers. The village of **Lower Largo** had a famous son in the form of Alexander Selkirk, whose adventures (see page 82) were the inspiration for Daniel Defoe's novel *Robinson Crusoe*. The cottage where he was born is marked by a statue of Selkirk as Crusoe.

South to the Borders

To the south of Edinburgh lies the Border Country, a land of castles and abbeys, mill towns, and market towns, in times past a battlefield for the Scots and the English, and forever linked with the 19th century novelist Sir Walter Scott.

The road towards Jedburgh and Newcastle cuts through the hills of the Southern Uplands, following the valley of Leader Water. Near the village of Lauder is **Thirlestane Castle**, an ancient stronghold on the invasion route from England. Dating from the 13th century, it was rebuilt during the 16th and 17th centuries for the Maitland family, the earls of Lauderdale. The staterooms preserve some of the finest Restoration plasterwork in existence, while the nursery has fascinating antique toys. Open May-June and September 2.00-4.30 P.M. (closed Tuesday, Friday, and Saturday); open July-August Sunday-Thursday noon-4:30 P.M.

A side road from the village of Earlston leads to a viewpoint above a bend in the River Tweed, named **Scott's View.** This was one of Sir Walter's favourite spots, with a vista across the river to the triple summits of the Eildon Hills. On his death in 1832 he was buried at **Dryburgh Abbey,** a little further south. Founded in 1150, the abbey was destroyed by the English in 1322, 1385, and in the "Rough Wooing" of 1544, after which it was never rebuilt. Although the church is ruined, the monastic buildings nearby are some of the best-preserved in the country. Sir Walter Scott's tomb is in the north transept of the church.

At Melrose, just to the west, is another great monastic ruin. **Melrose Abbey** was founded by David I in 1136, and it too was razed by English invaders in 1385; the present ruins date mainly from the 15th century. Its elegant Gothic architecture was the inspiration for George Meikle Kemp's design of the Scott Monument (see page 55).

Both abbeys are open from April to September 9:30 A.M.-6:30 P.M. (from 2:00 P.M. Sunday) and October to March 9:30 A.M.-4:30 P.M. (from 2:00 P.M. Sunday).

In 1811 Sir Walter Scott bought a farmhouse between Galashiels and Melrose, and over the years replaced it with the mansion of **Abbotsford,** where he lived until his death in 1832. The house stands as a monument to the imagination of Scotland's historical novelist. The building borrows its architectural details from various Scottish sources, including Roslin Chapel and Melrose Abbey, and the collection inside is equally eclectic—here is Rob Roy's Sword, a lock of Bonnie Prince Charlie's hair, and a painting of Mary Queen of Scots' severed head. Open mid-March to October 10:00 A.M.-5:00 P.M. (from 2:00 P.M. Sunday).

The Real Crusoe

Alexander Selkirk was born in 1676, the son of a Largo shoemaker. At the age of 19 he ran away to sea, and fell in with a crew of buccaneers. In 1704, following a quarrel with his captain, he asked to be put ashore on an uninhabited island in the Pacific 640 km (397 miles) west of Santiago, Chile. There he stayed, alone, for five years, until he was picked up by a passing British ship. Several accounts of his adventures were published, and inspired Defoe to write Robinson Crusoe. Selkirk, unable to adjust to life at home, took ship again, and died at sea in 1721. The islands where he was cast away have been renamed Isla Robinson Crusoe and Isla Alejandro Selkirk.

WHAT TO DO

THE FESTIVAL

When Edinburgh people speak of "The Festival," they usually mean the period of three or four weeks during August and early September when there are actually several separate events running simultaneously. The Jazz Festival, the Film Festival, and the Book Festival all take place around this time, in addition to the main Arts Festival, the Fringe, and the Military Tattoo. During these weeks Edinburgh's population doubles as some 500,000 visitors descend on the city to enjoy the numerous delights on offer. Any kind of accommodation is at a premium, and hotels are booked up many months in advance.

Edinburgh International Festival

The main festival, and the one that started it all, is the Edinburgh International Festival of the Arts. The first, comparatively modest Edinburgh Festival took place in 1947; since then it has grown to be one of the world's biggest, most exciting celebrations of the arts, with performances of theatre, opera, music, and dance by leading companies from all around the world. The dates of the Festival vary a little from year to year, but it generally runs for the last two weeks of August and the first week of September. One of the biggest annual attractions is the Bank of Scotland Fireworks Concert, held in the Ross Bandstand in Princes Street Gardens on the last Thursday of the Festival, when Edinburgh Castle provides the backdrop for one of the world's most spectacular displays of pyrotechnics.

The Festival programme is available from late March each year, and the Box Office is open for bookings from mid-April onwards, at 21 Market Street, Edinburgh EH1 1BW, tel. (0131) 473 2000.

The Festival Fringe

When the very first Edinburgh Festival was held, a few theatre companies that had not managed to get into the programme grouped together to form their own mini-festival, called the Fringe. Thus began a "sideshow" that has grown and grown into an annual extravaganza that today eclipses the official festival in terms of size and turnover, with some 1,000 shows at more than 130 venues, selling nearly half a million tickets each year. The world's largest arts festival offers an enormous range of entertainment — everything from stand-up comedy, drama, rock music, and cabaret, to circus acts, street theatre, mime, poetry, dance, jazz, and children's shows. Nowadays, the Fringe runs concurrently with the official festival.

Mound Place becomes a huge stage for buskers, jugglers, and fire-eaters at festival time.

The Fringe programme appears in late June each year, and from July onwards the Fringe Box Office is open for bookings at 180 High Street, Edinburgh EH1 1QS, tel. (0131) 226 5257/5259. During the festival, you'll also find a free Fringe Daily Diary available, detailing the times and venues of all the shows and events taking place that day.

Edinburgh Military Tattoo

The Military Tattoo is an annual military spectacular, held on the Esplanade with the castle as a backdrop. The show includes marvellous displays by military motorcycle and gymnastics teams, in addition to the all-important marching and music from military bands—featuring the popular massed pipes and drums. It finishes with a moving lament played by a lone piper standing on the battlements. The tattoo is usually held during the last three weeks of August.

The Tattoo Box Office is open for telephone bookings and general enquiries from January to July, at 33-34 Market Street, Edinburgh EH1 QB; tel. (0131) 225 1188, counter sales from July, at the Tattoo Ticket Sales Office, 31/33 Waverley Bridge.

SHOPPING

Edinburgh's main shopping area is situated along Princes Street and George Street and the little lanes and streets that lie between them. One side of Princes Street is lined with well-known shops, whilst the other side is free of buildings, allowing shoppers to enjoy an unobstructed view of the castle and the Old Town. Jenners, the "grand old man" of Princes Street, is the world's oldest independent department store, on the corner of South St. Andrew Street. On Rose Street and its lanes there are more individual shops selling crafts, clothes, shoes, and sporting goods. The Royal Mile is the place for gifts and

The Fringe Daily Diary can help plan which of the many shows to see.

the Waverley Market, with its many specialist shops and chain stores, is an attractive place to stroll around. The indoor shopping complex at St. James centre houses the well-known department store John Lewis. For more unusual shops, antiques stores, and speciality boutiques, head for Victoria Street and the Grassmarket, or try St. Stephen's Street in Stockbridge.

Woollens. Quality knitwear made from Scottish wool is always one of the most popular souvenirs, and deservedly so. Fine lambswool pullovers and cardigans in Fair Isle and Shetland patterns, as well as skirts, scarves, and golfing sweaters, can all be found in the numerous woollen shops on Princes Street and the Royal Mile. There are also kilts and jackets and hand-woven Harris tweed from the Outer Hebrides.

Tartan. A popular service offered by a number of Edinburgh's woollen shops is the clan tartan search. Your surname is entered into a computer, which informs you which Scottish clan (if any) you are affiliated to, and which tartans your name entitles you to wear. You can then, if you like, have a kilt (or any other item of clothing) made to order in your own clan tartan. Try the Clan Tartan Centre at the Pringle Woollen Mill in Leith, tel. (0131) 553 5161.

Calendar of Events

Remember that the timing of events may change from year to year. Check with the local tourist office to confirm exact dates.

April: *Edinburgh International Science Festival*: promoting science for all, with exhibitions, talks, hands-on workshops, family shows, theatre, and more. A different theme each year.

June: *Royal Highland Show*: Scotland's biggest agricultural fair, with flower shows, a craft fair, displays of food and drink, competitions. Held at Ingliston, just west of the city.

August: *Edinburgh Military Tattoo:* one of the city's biggest attractions, a wonderfully spectacular military display performed against the backdrop of the castle, with massed pipe bands and the famous lone piper. (See page 85)

Edinburgh International Jazz Festival: a week-long celebration of jazz, with big-name performers from all over the world, and live music from lunchtime until late at night.

Edinburgh International Film Festival: a major event, showing the best of new cinema from numerous countries around the world, plus U.K. premieres and gala performances.

Bank of Scotland Fireworks Concert: last Thursday of the Festival in August. The castle is backdrop for a spectacular pyrotechnics display, set to classical music played live at the Ross Bandstand.

August-September: *Edinburgh International Festival:* one of the world's most famous arts festivals, offering three weeks of top class music, ballet, opera, and theatre. (See page 83)

Festival Fringe: the world's biggest arts festival. Three weeks of magic and mayhem, with drama, comedy, music, dance, street entertainment, circus, and much more. (See page 84)

30-31 December: *Hogmanay Celebrations:* the traditional Scottish New Year celebrations are accompanied by concerts, street entertainment, and a torchlit procession from Parliament Square to a huge bonfire on top of Calton Hill.

Crafts. Scotland's numerous artisans produce a wide range of traditional handicrafts, including jewellery (especially silver), enamel ware, ceramics, pottery, textiles, and even replica antique weapons such as traditional Highland dirks and claymores. A showcase for local craftspeople to display their work is provided by the Scottish Craft Centre, 328 Lawnmarket, Royal Mile, tel. (0131) 225 4152.

Glassware. Edinburgh has a long tradition of glass-making, and the city still produces top-quality crystal ware. You can watch glass-blowers at work at the Edinburgh Crystal Visitor Centre at Eastfield, Penicuik, 16 km (10 miles) south of Edinburgh, tel. (01968) 675 128.

Jewellery and silverware. Scottish jewellery is renowned for its high quality of workmanship. Scottish silver and native semi-precious stone like cairngorm, carnelian and agate are worked into attractive designs, many based on ancient Celtic

and Pictish patterns. Other traditional silver objects include the *skean dhu* (ornamental dagger), the kilt pin, and the *quaich* (a two-handled drinking bowl).

Books. Edinburgh's confirmed position as one of the leading centres of learning in Europe means that it is something of a mecca for bookworms. The local firm James Thin runs Scotland's

Edinburgh's large department stores are made for the serious shopper.

largest bookshop at 57 George Street. Other major bookstores include Waterstones on George Street and also Princes Street, and Bauermeister on George IV Bridge. In addition, you'll find countless excellent second-hand and antiquarian bookshops—you might like to try scanning the shelves at Old Grindle's in Spittal Street, Grant & Shaw and Peter Bell in the West Port, and Castle Books on the Canongate, all of which have good titles relating to Edinburgh and Scotland

Tiny antiques shops have their own kind of charm to offer visitors.

ENTERTAINMENT

There is no shortage of entertainment in Edinburgh. Information on current events can be found in the free monthly publication *Edinburgh Day-by-Day*, available from the Information Centre (see TOURIST INFORMATION OFFICES on page 122). More detailed listings, including features and reviews, can be found in *The List* magazine (see page 116).

Music. A regular programme of classical concerts, opera, ballet, and various musical entertainments is performed in the Usher Hall, the Queen's Hall, and the Playhouse. Major rock concerts are usually held in the Playhouse. Live rock, folk, and jazz music can be enjoyed in many of the city's pubs and clubs—listings are provided in *The Gig Guide*, distributed free in participating pubs. The addresses and telephone numbers of the principal city venues are as follows: Usher Hall, Lothian Road, tel. (0131) 228 8616; Queen's Hall, Clerk Street, tel. (0131) 668 2019; The Playhouse, 18-22 Greenside Place, tel. (0131) 557 2590.

Theatre. Edinburgh contains a wide array of lively theatres, offering visitors a year-round programme of drama, dance, musicals, comedies, and pantomime. The mainstream theatres include the Festival, the Lyceum, and the King's. The Traverse is famous for its support of new and experimental works. Addresses for these particular theatres are as follows: Royal Lyceum, Grindlay Street, tel. (0131) 229 9697; King's Theatre, 2 Leven Street, tel. (0131) 229 1201; Traverse Theatre, Cambridge Street, tel. (0131) 228 1404.

Cinema. Film enthusiasts are well catered for in Edinburgh, which has several major cinemas. Lothian Road, at the west end of Princes Street, has three cinemas within five minutes' walk of one another. The Filmhouse screens art-house films, foreign films, and reruns of popular classics. The MGM is a mainstream first-run house. The Cameo, a little further on in Tollcross, has a mixed programme, and offers a good selection of late-night shows on Thursday, Friday, and Saturday.

The famous Traverse Theatre is now housed in a new building next to Usher Hall.

SPORTS

Edinburgh and the surrounding region offer a wide range of sports and leisure activities. Detailed information on individual activities can be obtained from the Edinburgh and Scotland Information Centre (see TOURIST INFORMATION OFFICES on page 122), while the Scottish Tourist Board provides details of facilities throughout the country, including separate booklets for golf, angling, hill-walking, cycling, and a number of watersports.

Golf: Edinburgh has a very long association with golf, dating right back to the origins of the game—Leith Links (see page 59) claims to be the "Home of Golf." There are six municipal courses, open every day of the year except Christmas Day, and a further 70 or so within 32 km (20 miles) of the city centre. The world-famous Old Course at St. Andrews (see page 79) is only 88 km (55 miles) from the centre of Edinburgh, making it easily accessible for a day excursion.

Angling: Within the city limits, you can fish for brown trout in the Water of Leith, or for pike, perch, and roach in the Union Canal. There are many well-stocked rivers, lochs, and reservoirs within easy reach of Edinburgh and, in the outer reaches of the Firth of Forth, there is good sea-angling. Details of permits and boat hire can be obtained at the Information Centre (see TOURIST INFORMATION OFFICES on page 122). The booklet, *Freshwater Fishing in the Lothian Region*, is available in bookshops.

Walking: There are many fine walks to be enjoyed in and around Edinburgh, both long and short, easy and strenuous. You can try a leisurely stroll along the Water of Leith Walkway, the Union Canal towpath, or the Hermitage of Braid, or for a more strenuous expedition, climb to the summit of Arthur's Seat or explore the ridges of the Pentland Hills.

Cycling: Edinburgh is nowadays crisscrossed by a network of cycle paths that follow the routes of abandoned railway lines; many continue beyond the city boundary, and lead you into lovely countryside. There are also mountain-bike routes through the valleys of the Pentland Hills. A helpful map of the city's cycle routes, published by *Spokes*, is available from the Information Centre and bike shops.

Horseback riding: There are several stables that offer guided treks and hired mounts.

Watersports: Swimming centres include the big Commonwealth Pool, tel. (0131) 667 7211, which has a 50-metre swimming pool, a diving pool, and a children's pool; and Leith Waterworld, tel. (0131) 555 6000. Port Edgar Marina at Queensferry offers windsurfing, canoe and sailing dinghy instruction and hire, tel. (0131) 331 3330.

Skiing and Paragliding: Europe's longest artificial ski slope is at the Hillend Ski Centre, on the northern slopes of the Pentland Hills, tel. (0131) 445 4433. It is open all year, and provides equipment hire and tuition. The ski resorts of Cairngorm, Glenshee, Glencoe, and Nevis Range, are all within three hours' drive of the city (season December-April). Also at Hillend is the Scottish Parapente Centre (paragliding) tel. (0131) 445 4995.

Spectator sports: Edinburgh has two Premier Division football (soccer) clubs—Heart of Midlothian and Hibernian—who play regular Saturday and Wednesday matches. The football grounds are at Tynecastle (Hearts), on Gorgie Road, and Easter Road (Hibs), north of London Road. Rugby Union matches are played at Murrayfield Stadium, on Corstorphine Road, during the Five Nations Championship (from January to March); athletics meetings are at Meadowbank Stadium, on London Road; horse racing is at Musselburgh, to the east.

Many boys in Edinburgh dream of following their rugby heroes onto the hallowed turf of Murrayfield.

EDINBURGH FOR CHILDREN

Edinburgh is one of Scotland's most child-friendly cities. Special provisions for younger visitors include baby-changing facilities, push-chair hire, playgrounds, and children's areas in bars and restaurants. When the sun shines, you can play on the sandy beach at Portobello, fly kites in Holyrood Park, take a boat trip to Inchcolm Island, or watch the Penguin Parade at Edinburgh Zoo (see page 68). At festival time, there are scores of circuses, street entertainers (head for the foot of the Mound, halfway along Princes Street), juggling, and face painting workshops.

Attractions for a rainy day include the Museum of Childhood (see page 43), the Camera Obscura (see page 39), some wonderful water slides at the Commonwealth Pool (see page 92), and Deep Sea World at North Queensferry (see page 70). For further information, ask for a free copy of the booklet *Child-Friendly Edinburgh* at the Information Centre.

EATING OUT

Edinburgh is very well provided with eating places, ranging from the most humble sandwich stalls to internationally renowned five-star restaurants. You can choose from a wide range of ethnic cuisines, including Thai, Indonesian, Moroccan, Mexican, and Creole, as well as the ubiquitous Italian, Indian, and Chinese. You will also find many Edinburgh restaurants specializing in fine traditional Scottish fare—such as lamb, venison, potatoes, oatmeal, herring, salmon, and seafood—using imaginative, French-inspired recipes. In the city centre, head for the Pompadour Room in the Caledonian Hotel, or try Stac Polly, Howie's, or The Witchery (see page 135). Out of town, both the Waterside at Haddington and the Champany's Inn near Linlithgow are famous for their excellent menus, while the Cellar Restaurant (across the Forth in Anstruther, Fife) serves up the finest seafood in the country.

As the sun begins to warm the city in summer-time, Grassmarket restaurants spill onto the street.

Vegetarians are reasonably well catered for. Most places now include at least one or two vegetarian dishes on the menu, and you'll find an increasing number of purely vegetarian restaurants—try the fresh salads and soups at Henderson's (see page 134) and Anna Purna (see page 132).

There are numerous guides to eating out in Edinburgh, including the *Edinburgh Food Guide* (available from the Information Centre—see page 122), and the *Taste of Scotland* programme, a Scottish Tourist Board initiative which recommends restaurants that make good use of traditional Scottish produce. The local events magazine *The List* (see page 116) also publishes an *Eating and Drinking Guide* listing restaurants, pubs, and cafés in and around Edinburgh.

Meal Times

Outside of hotels, **breakfast** is served in a number of cafés and bistros from around 8:00 A.M. Two attractive spots where you can linger over the morning paper while tucking into a traditional Scottish breakfast, or simply coffee and croissants, are the Caledonian Ale House at Haymarket (open 8:30 A.M. onwards), and Montpeliers in Morningside (open from 9:00 A.M.). Many pubs offer brunch on Saturday and Sunday, usually served between 10:30 A.M. and 3:00 or 4:00 P.M.; you can always enjoy a good, hearty fry-up at Biddy Mulligan's in the Grassmarket, Bannerman's in the Cowgate, Braidwood's in the West Port, and Maison Hector in Stockbridge, for example.

Pubs are a good bet for **lunch** as well. Many establishments in the centre offer bar lunches at extremely competitive prices, usually between noon and 2:30 P.M. However, if you want to avoid crowds of office workers, try to get in before 1:00 P.M. or after 2:00 P.M. A number of restaurants also offer good value "business" lunches from Monday to Friday, with a set meal of three courses costing as little as £5 to £7 a head.

Restaurants generally open for **dinner** around 6:00 or 7:00 P.M., and stop serving around 10:30 or 11:00 P.M., though many Indian, Italian, and Chinese restaurants may well stay open until after midnight (Lothian Road is famous for its late-night restaurants). If you want to be sure of getting a table on a Friday or a Saturday evening, you would do well to make a reservation a few days beforehand. Restaurants close to theatres such as Stac Polly (see page 135) often provide an attractive pre- or post-theatre dinner, offering a set menu at a fixed price—considerably cheaper than dining *à la carte*.

Breakfast in hotels is generally served from 7:00 to 9:00 A.M. Monday to Saturday, and 8:00 to 10:00 A.M. Sunday. The traditional Scottish breakfast is a hearty affair, consisting of porridge (hot oatmeal, served with milk or cream and a

Leith's Waterfront bistro offers a lovely atmosphere and fresh meals from the sea.

touch of salt—sugar is frowned upon!), followed by a plate of bacon, black pudding, potato scones, eggs, and toast, washed down with hot tea. A very popular alternative is a pair of kippers (smoked herring) with bread and butter. Many bars now serve a traditional breakfast as Sunday brunch, available from 10:00 A.M. to 3:00 P.M.

Scottish seafood is some of the best in the world.

Soups and Main Courses

Soups and broths, especially warming on a winter's day, are served in most Scottish restaurants. **Scotch broth** is a vegetable soup made with mutton stock, and thickened with barley and lentils, while **cock-a-leekie** is a tasty chicken soup flavoured with leeks. Two delicious seafood soups worth trying are **partan bree** (cream of crab), and **cullen skink** (made with smoked haddock, milk, onion, and potato).

Traditional Scottish produce used in main course dishes includes Aberdeen Angus beef, Scotch lamb, venison, grouse, salmon, trout, and seafood. These are either served simply, or with a sauce that makes use of local ingredients such as whisky, Drambuie, honey, and cream, accompanied by potatoes and vegetables. Seafood is especially good, with wonderful lobster, crab, langoustines, oysters, and scallops frequently on the menu.

The smokehouse has for centuries been used as a way of preserving fish and meat, and is making something of a comeback, with a number of small, independent businesses nowadays producing kippers, smoked mackerel, haddock, salmon, and venison. Kippers are smoked herring, while "Arbroath Smokies" and "Finnan Haddies" are smoked haddock, the former smoked over oak chips, the latter over peat.

No discussion of Scottish food would be complete without a mention of **haggis.** This famous dish is made by first mincing the heart, lungs, and liver of a sheep, mixing in oatmeal, onion, and seasoning, then stuffing the mixture into a sheep's stomach bag and finally boiling it for a couple of hours. It may sound disgusting, but it's actually very good, a spicy and savoury mince traditionally served with "bashed neeps and chappit tatties" — mashed turnips and mashed potatoes. It forms the centrepiece of any "Burns Supper," a dinner celebrating the poet Robert Burns, held annually on 25 January, the anniversary of his birth.

Desserts

Desserts are by no means an afterthought, for the Scots are renowned for having a sweet tooth, and nearly all Scottish menus offer a wide selection of cakes and puddings. Better quality restaurants also produce lighter desserts using traditionally Scottish fruits like raspberries, brambles, gooseberries, and rhubarb, and fine oatmeal and cream dishes such as **Cranachan** (cream, raspberries, and toasted oatmeal), and **Atholl brose** (a blend of cream, whisky, honey, and oatmeal). Scottish cheeses are also delicious, and go particularly well with locally produced oatcakes.

Drinks

The most famous Scottish drink, of course, is **whisky** (the name derives from the Gaelic *uisge beatha*, meaning "water of life"). There is a very important distinction between blended whiskies and "single malts." The single malt is distilled purely from malted barley, and is usually aged in oak sherry casks, producing a distinctively flavoured spirit, each as individual as a fine wine—and there are more than 100 brands to choose from. Blended whiskies, on the other hand, are produced by mixing different varieties of grain whisky (distilled from grains other than malted barley) and adding smaller amounts of malt whiskies. Blended whiskies are less expensive and less distinctive than malts, and are often used in mixed drinks; the only thing that should ever be added to a malt whisky is a splash of Highland spring water.

Sometimes overlooked by the visitor are the fine **beers** that are brewed in Scotland—many of them in Edinburgh. The city's Caledonian Brewery produces a wide range of excellent beers, including IPA (India Pale Ale) and the darker and noticeably stronger 80/- (Eighty Shilling—some Scottish beers are called 60/-, 70/-, and 80/- in order of increasing strength, a reference to the amount of excise duty that was once charged on each barrel). Caledonian Brewery also offers Golden Promise, a bottled organic beer that is regularly praised by food and drink writers. Most of Edinburgh's **pubs** are open from 11:00 A.M. to 11:00 P.M. every day, with many staying open until midnight or 1:00 A.M. from Monday to Saturday.

Connoisseurs of fine **wines** are well catered for in the city's more expensive restaurants, whose cellars offer a broad range of excellent vintages from France, Italy, Australia, California, as well as numerous other countries. Inevitably, you'll find the choice becomes more limited towards the lower end of the market, but here a house white and a house red are nearly always available, in both half- and one-litre carafes. Some smaller establishments that do not possess a drinks licence are happy for you to buy your own wine from a wine shop (generally open noon to 10:00 P.M. daily) and bring it along for the meal; they advertise themselves as "BYOB"—"bring your own bottle."

Edinburgh's Pubs

Edinburgh is a drinker's town, and it has long been famous for its historic pubs. The best-known "pub-crawls" are down the Royal Mile and along Rose Street, but there are many other fine bars to be explored in the West End, the Grassmarket, and Tollcross.

The Grassmarket contains a number of fine old *howffs* (drinking dens). **The Last Drop** is a low-ceilinged, atmospheric bar set in the ground floor of an Old Town tenement, and takes its name from the gallows that used to stand nearby—the "Last Drop" was not a drink, but a short and fatal journey. A wander down the dark defile of the Cowgate will lead you to the equally atmospheric cellars of **Bannerman's,** a warren of barrel-vaulted rooms buried beneath a pile of Old Town buildings. It's a lively bar with a mixed-age crowd, folk music in the evenings, and a famously good fried brunch served Saturdays and Sundays from 11:00 A.M. to 4:30 P.M.

You can enjoy a more sophisticated brunch of Bucks Fizz, oysters, and salmon at the **Café Royal Oyster Bar** in West Register Street (at the east end of Princes Street). Next door is the famous **Circle Bar,** a vast Victorian pub with marble floors, leather banquettes, highly polished brass rails, and an enormous oval island bar. One of the walls is dominated by huge Doulton tile portraits of James Watt, Michael Faraday, George Stephenson, and various other Victorian engineers and inventors.

Tucked away in Duddingston Village, at the foot of Arthur's Seat, is the 18th-century **Sheep Heid Inn,** which claims to be one of Scotland's oldest licensed premises (it takes its name from the Scots dish of sheep's-head broth which was once served to weary travellers). At the back of the pub is a traditional skittle alley, one of the few still in existence, which draws enthusiasts from far and wide.

Another traditional Scottish recreation is proudly celebrated in **The Golf Tavern,** also a pub with a remarkably long pedigree. It is set on the edge of Bruntsfield Links, where there has been an inn ever since the 15th century—King James III is said to have played a few rounds on the links before quenching his thirst in the tavern. The present building dates from the 19th century, and is comfortably furnished with welcoming leather sofas.

The Athletic Arms, on the corner of Henderson Terrace and Angle Park Terrace, has achieved near-mythical status amongst connoisseurs of fine ale. This beer-drinker's Mecca is better known as The Diggers—it was once a favourite haunt of the gravediggers who worked in the cemetery across the street. Foaming pints of McEwan's 80/- (Eighty Shilling) are dispensed from no less than eleven taps by a small army of red-jacketed barmen, who, with extraordinary efficiency, serve the crowds of football and rugby fans who gather here on match days. On occasions when the pub is busy, you don't even have to speak to order your beer— simply catch a barman's eye, and raise three fingers, and three pints will be placed in front of you (if you want something other than pints of 80/-, then you're in the wrong pub!).

Down in Leith, the **Waterfront Wine Bar** is one of the most popular eating and drinking establishments in Edinburgh's dockland. It is set in a wood-panelled dockside waiting room (note the nautical bric-a-brac and the old signs pointing the way to the ferry), and offers outside tables during summer, and an attractive conservatory during winter.

Another hostelry to look out for if you are by the waterfront is the **Hawes Inn** in Queensferry. This is an historic tavern, tucked underneath the southern end of the Forth Railway Bridge, which was made famous by Robert Louis Stevenson when he used it as a setting in his novel *Kidnapped*.

INDEX

HANDY TRAVEL TIPS

An A–Z Summary of Practical Information

A

ACCOMMODATION (See also CAMPING, YOUTH HOSTELS, and the list of RECOMMENDED HOTELS on page 129)

Edinburgh offers an extensive range of accommodation, from luxury hotels and historic houses, through slightly more modest hotels and boarding houses, to simple bed-and-breakfast establishments and backpackers' hostels.

Hotels and guest houses that have been inspected and approved by the Scottish Tourist Board (STB) are given gradings according to the facilities on offer (from one to five crowns) and also according to standards of service ("Approved," "Commended," or "Highly Commended.") The STB publishes an annually updated list of hotels, which includes full details of their prices and facilities (see Tourist Information Offices).

In the high season (July-September), and especially during the three weeks of the Edinburgh International Festival, Edinburgh becomes particularly crowded and accommodation is at a premium. Should you intend to visit during this period, you are strongly advised to book accommodation in the city as far in advance as possible. However, if you do find yourself in Edinburgh without a hotel reservation, head for one of the city's Tourist Information and Accommodation Centres, where the staff will generally try to find a room for you.

AIRPORT

Edinburgh Airport lies 11 km (6.5 miles) west of the city centre. Facilities include a self-service restaurant, bar, café, bank, currency exchange desk (open 6:00 A.M.-10:00 P.M.), tourist information desk, hotel reservations desk, and car rental desks.

For flight enquiries, contact one of the following numbers: British Airways, tel. 0345 222111 for sales and reservations, (0131) 344 3215 for inquiries; British Midland, tel. (0131) 344 33 02; Air UK, tel. (0131) 344 3325; or Servisair (for all other airlines), tel. (0131) 344 3111.

There are two bus services, the "Airporter" and the "Airbus Express," linking the airport with Waverley Bridge in central Edinburgh, which run between 7:20 A.M. and 10:30 P.M., with departures roughly every 15 minutes between 9:00 A.M. and 5:00 P.M. (journey time approximately 30 minutes). There is a taxi rank outside the terminal.

B

BICYCLE HIRE

Edinburgh is a bicycle-friendly city with many miles of traffic-free cycle tracks (maps available from any cycle shop). Both road bikes and mountain bikes can be hired from Central Cycle Hire, 13 Lochrin Place, Tollcross, tel. (0131) 228 6633.

The Scottish Tourist Board issues a free pamphlet which gives the addresses of bicycle rental firms.

C

CAMPING

There are a number of camping and caravan sites on the fringes of the city, but these are frequently booked up well in advance. The most convenient sites are Edinburgh Caravan Club, Marine Drive, tel. (0131) 312 6874; and Mortonhall Caravan Park, 38 Mortonhall Gate, Frogston Road East, tel. (0131) 664 1533. To camp or caravan on private land you need the owner's permission.

CAR HIRE (See also DRIVING IN SCOTLAND)

A car is more of a hindrance than a help in the traffic-choked streets of central Edinburgh. However, if you are planning to travel further afield, renting a car is an ideal way of exploring Scotland. A car gives you the freedom to travel at your own pace, and to explore places inaccessible by public transport. There are numerous car-hire firms in Edinburgh; rates vary considerably, and you should shop around for the lowest price. Check that the quoted rate includes Collision

Damage Waiver, unlimited mileage, and VAT, as these can greatly increase the cost.

You must be over 21 to hire a car, and need a full, valid driver's licence (EC model) which you have held for at least 12 months, and a major credit card—cash deposits are prohibitively large.

CLIMATE and CLOTHING

Edinburgh enjoys a climate that is drier than the west of Scotland, and thus sunnier in summer, but often colder in winter. When an easterly wind blows off the North Sea, a cold mist called the haar envelops the city. The best time to visit is in May and June, when rain is least likely and many flowers are in full bloom. In June, daylight lasts until after 10:00 P.M., and the sun is up by 4:00 A.M.; conversely, in December it is dark and gloomy, with daylight lasting only from 9:00 A.M. to 3:30 P.M. September is also good, though wetter than spring. You can get an up-to-date weather forecast for the area by telephoning 0891 505322. (Calls charged at 45p/50p a minute at cheap/normal rate.)

Average temperatures

	J	F	M	A	M	J	J	A	S	O	N	D
°C	3	3	4	7	10	13	15	14	12	9	6	4
°F	37	37	39	45	50	55	59	58	54	48	43	39

Rainfall

(mm)	71	56	51	43	66	51	81	84	69	84	74	61
(inches)	2.8	2.2	2.0	1.7	2.6	2.0	3.2	3.3	2.7	3.3	2.9	2.4

Clothing. No matter what time of the year, you will need rainwear and warm clothes. It can be hot in July and August, but not for long. Good walking shoes are strongly recommended for exploring Edinburgh's hilly and cobbled streets.

COMMUNICATIONS
(See also OPENING HOURS and TIME DIFFERENCES)

Post Offices. Post offices are indicated by a red sign with yellow lettering, and there are many scattered throughout the city. Opening hours are 9:00 A.M.-5:30 P.M. Monday to Friday; 9:00 A.M.-12:30 P.M. Saturday. The Head Post Office is at 2-4 Waterloo Place, Edinburgh EH1 1AA, at the east end of Princes Street, open 8:30 A.M.-6:00 P.M. Monday to Friday; 8:30 A.M.-12:30 P.M. Saturday.

Mail to addresses within the UK can be sent first class (usually delivered next day) or second class (may take two to five days). Letters up to 60*g* within the U.K., or up to 20*g* within the EC (all EC letters go by airmail), cost 25p by first class. Telegrams no longer exist in the U.K.; the equivalent is a Telemessage (see Telephones, below).

You can have mail addressed to you c/o Poste Restante at the Head Post Office; to collect it, you will need to show your passport or driver's licence as identification.

Telephones/faxes. There are abundant public telephones in street booths, in pubs and restaurants, bus and railway stations, and other public buildings. All of them can be used to make local or international calls. Coin-operated phones accept all coins except 1p; booths with a green "Cardphone" sign take a telephone card, available from post offices and newsagents in £1, £5, and £10 denominations; some others accept credit cards and charge cards. Instructions for use are clearly displayed inside the booth.

If you know the name and address of the person you want to call, but not their number, dial 192 for Directory Enquiries.

To make a long-distance telephone call within the U.K., dial the area code followed by the number. To make a local call, dial only the number. The area code for Edinburgh is 0131.

To make an international call, dial 00, followed by the appropriate country code (1 for U.S.A. and Canada, 61 for Australia, 64 for New Zealand, 27 for South Africa), then the number.

To call an operator in your home country, dial 0800 89, followed by 0064 (New Zealand Direct); 0061 (OTC Australia Direct); 0016 (Canada Direct); 0011 (U.S.A. AT&T); 0222 (U.S.A. MCI); 0456 (U.S.A. TRT); or 0877 (U.S.A. Sprint Express). For International Operator, dial 155; for International Directory Enquiries, dial 153.

Faxes can be sent from one of the many fax bureaux in the city centre. A **Telemessage** (the modern equivalent of a telegram) must be dictated over the phone, by dialling 0800 190190.

COMPLAINTS

Complaints should be addressed to the management of the hotel, restaurant, or shop involved. If you are not satisfied, you can report the matter to the Edinburgh Tourist Board (see TOURIST INFORMATION BOARDS) or Lothian Regional Council Advice Shop, 85/87 South Bridge, tel. (0131) 225 1255.

CRIME (See also EMERGENCIES and POLICE)

The centre of Edinburgh is fairly safe compared to other large European cities. All the same, you should take the usual precautions against theft—don't carry large amounts of cash; leave your valuables in the hotel safe, not in your room; and beware of pickpockets in crowded areas. Never leave your bags or valuables on view in a parked car—take them with you or lock them in the trunk. Any theft or loss must be reported immediately to the police in order to comply with your travel insurance. If your passport is lost or stolen, you should also inform your consulate.

CUSTOMS and ENTRY FORMALITIES

All visitors to the U.K. need a valid passport, except for citizens of E.C. countries, for whom an identity card will suffice. The United Kingdom and the Republic of Ireland comprise a single customs zone —you do not need to clear customs when travelling between the two.

Visas. Citizens of the Commonwealth and of the U.S.A. are not required to obtain a visa for stays of up to six months. Travellers of other nationalities should first check visa requirements with their nearest British Embassy.

Note that visa regulations change from time to time, and should be confirmed through your travel agent.

Currency restrictions. There are no limits on the amount of currency you can take into or out of the country.

As the U.K. is part of the EU, free exchange of non-duty free goods for personal use is permitted between EU countries and the U.K. However, exchange of duty free items is still subject to restrictions, so check before you go.

Restrictions on bringing duty free items obtained outside the EU are: 200 cigarettes or 50 cigars or 250*g* tobacco; 2*l* still table wine and 1*l* spirits or 2*l* fortified wine.

Returning to your own country, restrictions are: Australia: 250 cigarettes or 250*g* tobacco; 1*l* alcohol; Canada: 200 cigarettes and 50 cigars and 400*g* tobacco; 1.1*l* spirits or wine or 8.5*l* beer; New Zealand: 200 cigarettes or 50 cigars or 250*g* tobacco; 4.5*l* wine or beer and 1.1*l* spirits; South Africa: 400 cigarettes and 50 cigars and 250*g* tobacco; 2*l* wine and 1*l* spirits; U.S.A.: 200 cigarettes and 100 cigars or a "reasonable amount" of tobacco.

D

DRIVING IN SCOTLAND (See also CAR HIRE)

If you plan to bring your own vehicle into the U.K., you will also need to bring your registration and insurance papers, and a valid driving licence (the majority of foreign licences can be used in the U.K. for up to twelve months).

Driving conditions. The general rule is drive on the left, pass on the right—note that passing on the inside is illegal. Speed limits are generally displayed in miles per hour. Unless indicated otherwise, these are 48 kph (30 mph) within built-up areas, 98 kph (60 mph) on single-carriageway main roads, and 120 kph (70 mph) on dual carriageways and motorways. Seat belts are compulsory for driver and all passengers, back seat included.

Driving conditions are generally good, except in the major cities, where congestion is a problem. In the northwest Highlands and the Hebrides many roads are single-track and unfenced, and livestock wandering onto the road can be a hazard. Passing places should be used to allow cars behind you to pass.

In winter, all regions of the country can be affected by snow and ice, and roads over high ground are occasionally blocked by snow.

Edinburgh is surrounded by a ringroad, which allows through traffic to bypass the city centre; there are motorway connections to Glasgow (M8), Stirling (M9), and Perth (M90). The left-hand lane of a number of the city's principal streets is marked off as a bus lane—these are reserved for buses only during the periods 8:30-9:15 A.M. and 4:30-6:00 P.M., Monday to Friday.

Petrol/gasoline. There are numerous petrol (gas) stations on the main roads in and out of the city, and several are close to the city centre; most petrol stations are open 24 hours a day.

Fluid measures

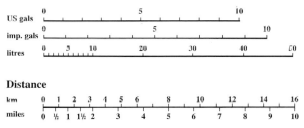

Distance

Parking. Daytime city centre parking is expensive, and finding a space on the street can be a problem (maximum stay 1 or 2 hours). Most street parking is "pay-and-display"—you buy a ticket from a machine and display it in the windscreen. Don't park in spaces marked "Permit Holders Only." It's cheaper and easier to use one of the off-street car parks, where you pay on exit—the main ones are at Castle Terrace (below the Castle) and the St. James Centre (top of Leith Walk, at the east end of Princes Street).

Edinburgh

Breakdown. If your car breaks down, and you are not a member of the AA (0800) 887 766 or RAC, you will have to call out a mechanic. There are a number of Edinburgh garages that offer 24-hour recovery services—try Barlas Recovery, tel. (0131) 669 6867/5891, or Rosebank Recovery, tel. (0131) 449 4420. If your car is rented, call the number in the hire documents (most hire companies have membership in the AA or RAC).

E

ELECTRIC CURRENT

240V/50Hz AC is standard; sockets are three-pin. You will need an adaptor for foreign appliances, as well as a transformer for American 110V equipment.

EMBASSIES and CONSULATES

All foreign embassies are located in London, but some countries maintain consulates in Scotland. Check their hours first by phone.

Australian Consulate: Call (0171) 379 4334

U.S. Consulate: 3 Regent Terrace, Edinburgh EH7 5BN, tel. (0131) 556 8315.

EMERGENCIES (See also MEDICAL CARE)

In an emergency, you can call free from any public telephone—dial 999 and ask for the service you require.

Police	**999**
Ambulance	**999**
Fire	**999**
Coast-guard	**999**

G

GAY & LESBIAN TRAVELLERS

Edinburgh has a lively gay scene and there are several gay pubs and discos in the centre. The best place to find out details of what's on is the Blue Moon Café, 36 Broughton Street, P.O. Box 169, Edinburgh EH1 3UU, (0131) 557 0911, at the east end of town. The café basement also houses a Lesbian and Gay Community Centre, from where the Edinburgh Gay Switchboard is run, tel. (0131) 556 4049 (lines open 7:30 A.M.-10:00 P.M.). A gay bookshop, the West and Wilde, is at 25a Dundas Street (0131) 556 0079.

GUIDES and TOURS

There are many companies and individuals offering all kinds of guided tours of Edinburgh. One of the most popular is the open-top bus tour of the city, which leaves regularly from Waverley Bridge. Your ticket is valid all day, and you can get off anywhere you like and then join a later bus for the rest of the tour. There are many others—personalized taxi tours of the city, coach tours to outlying attractions, self-guided audio tours, historical walks, and night-time walking tours of the Old Town's haunted closes. For full details, contact tourist information.

L

LANGUAGE

Just because you speak English, you're certainly not home Scot-free in Scotland. Gaelic and old Scots words and phrases will baffle the most fluent English speaker. Today just over 82,000 Scots speak Gaelic, though most of them live in the Western Isles. However, many place names throughout the country are derived from Gaelic names, and words and phrases from the old Scots dialect called "Lallans" are still in common use. Even "normal" English, spoken with a strong Scottish accent, can take a while to get used to. Here are some examples to help you along.

Scottish/Gaelic	*English*
auld lang syne	days long ago
Auld Reekie	Edinburgh (Old Smoky)
aye	yes
bairn	child
ben	mountain
bide a wee	wait a bit
biggin	building
bonny/bonnie	pretty
brae	hillside
bramble	blackberry
brig	bridge
burn	stream
cairn	pile of stones
ceilidh	song/story gathering
clachan	hamlet
croft	small land-holding
dinna fash yersel'	don't get upset
dram	measure of Scotch
firth	estuary
ghillie	attendant for hunting or fishing
glen	valley
haud yer wheesht	shut up
Hogmanay	New Year's Eve
inver	mouth of river
ken	know
kirk	church
knock	knoll
kyle	strait
lang may yer lum reek	long may your chimney smoke (i.e. may you have a long life)
lassie	girl

links	seaside golf course
linn	waterfall
loch	lake
mickle (as in: **many a mickle maks a muckle**)	small amount (little things add up to big things)
mull	promontory
provost	mayor
sett	tartan pattern
skirl	sound of bagpipes
strath	river valley
thunderplump	thunderstorm
tolbooth	old courthouse/jail
wean	child
wee	small
wynd	lane

LAUNDRY and DRY CLEANING

Your hotel will be able to provide a laundry service, but it is usually faster and cheaper to use one of the many coin-operated launderettes where you can wash your clothes yourself.

In most launderettes you can choose, for a small extra charge, a "service wash"—drop off your laundry in the morning, and collect it in the afternoon, washed, dried, and folded.

LOST PROPERTY (See also CRIME)

Items that have been found and handed in to the police can be picked up at the Police HQ in Fettes Avenue. For missing items that may have been left behind on public transport, contact the relevant company (listed opposite) and ask for the Lost Property Office.

Police Lost Property Office, tel. (0131) 311 3141

Waverley Railway Station, tel. (0131) 556 2477.

St. Andrew Square Bus Station, tel. (0131) 557 5061.

Lothian Regional Transport (buses), tel. (0131) 554 4494.

M

MEDIA

Radio. Local radio stations in the area include BBC Radio Scotland (FM 92.4/94.7 MHz, AM 810 KHz), with Scottish and international news, features, and current affairs; and Forth FM (97.3 MHz), for pop music, local news, and traffic reports.

Television. Edinburgh receives four TV channels—two public service channels, BBC1 and BBC2, and two commercial channels, STV, and Channel 4. The main evening news programmes on BBC1 are at 6:00 P.M. and 9:00 P.M., both followed by a weather forecast; STV news is at 5:40 P.M. and 10:00 P.M.; Channel 4 news is at 7:00 P.M. Local news is on both BBC1 and STV at 6:30 P.M.

Newspapers. Scotland has two quality national daily papers, *The Herald* and *The Scotsman,* and one quality Sunday paper, *Scotland on Sunday.* The latter two, and the *Edinburgh Evening News,* are published in Edinburgh and include much useful information on restaurants, pubs, special events, and entertainment, as well as local, national, and international news and features.

A particularly useful listings magazine is *The List*, published every fortnight, which covers music, theatre, cinema, art, and sport in both Edinburgh and Glasgow.

MEDICAL CARE (See also EMERGENCIES)

Overseas visitors to the UK are entitled to free emergency treatment at hospital Accident and Emergency units. However, you should not leave home without an adequate medical insurance policy, preferably one that includes cover for an emergency flight home in the event of serious injury or illness. Your travel agent, bank, or insurance broker can provide a comprehensive policy that will cover not only medical costs, but also theft or loss of money and possessions, delayed or cancelled flights, and so on.

For minor ailments, you can seek advice from the local pharmacy, or chemist. These are usually open during normal shopping hours. After hours, at least one per town remains open all night; its location is posted in the window of all other pharmacies. (Boots the Chemist in Shandwick Place is open 8.45 A.M.-9:00 P.M. Monday-Saturday; 10:00 A.M.-5:00 P.M. Sunday). Alternatively, contact a local doctor; your hotel will have a list of available GPs.

For emergency dental treatment, contact the Edinburgh Dental Hospital, tel. (0131) 536 4900.

Vaccinations. There are no compulsory immunization requirements for entry into the U.K.

MONEY MATTERS (See also CUSTOMS AND ENTRY FORMALITIES)

Currency. The unit of currency in the U.K. is the pound sterling (£), equal to 100 pence (p). The Bank of England issues notes in denominations of £5, £10, £20, and £50, and coins of 1p, 2p, 5p, 10p, 20p, 50p, and £1.

The three main Scottish banks—the Bank of Scotland, the Royal Bank of Scotland, and the Clydesdale Bank—also issue their own distinctive banknotes, which are exactly equal in value to the Bank of England notes. In addition, the Royal Bank of Scotland continues to issue green £1 notes. (Travellers who take Scottish notes abroad may have trouble converting them to other currencies; they are also occasionally refused by shops in southern England.)

Banks and currency exchange offices. Banking hours are generally 9:30 A.M.-4:30 P.M. Monday to Friday. The Royal Bank of Scotland on North Bridge is open until 7:00 P.M. on Wednesday and Thursday, and opens 10:00 A.M.-4:00 P.M. on Saturday.

There are currency exchange desks at Edinburgh Airport and Waverley Station, and also in the American Express and Thomas Cook offices on Princes Street.

Credit cards, traveller's cheques. Major credit and charge cards are accepted by most shops, restaurants, hotels, petrol stations, and car hire companies—look for the signs in the window. The American Express office is at 139 Princes Street (west end), tel. (0131) 225 7881/9179.

Traveller's cheques are widely accepted throughout Edinburgh and Scotland. You will need your passport when you go to cash one.

PLANNING YOUR BUDGET

To give you an idea of what to expect, here's a list of typical prices.

Airport transfer. Airporter bus to/from Waverley Bridge £3, single, £5 return.

Bicycle hire. Around £35-60 a week, depending on model.

Buses. Adult fares 50p to 60p. One-day pass £2.20.

Camping. Around £6 to £10 per tent per night.

Car hire. Ford Fiesta £22 a day, plus 15p a mile after first 200 miles; £148 a week, unlimited mileage. Ford Sierra £49.50 a day, plus 15p a mile after first 200 miles; £290 a week, unlimited mileage.

Entertainment. Cinema £3.75-4.60; theatre £2.50-30.00; concert £3.00-15.00; nightclub £3.00-7.00.

Excursions. Open-top bus tour of Edinburgh, with commentary £7; walking tour of Old Town £5 per person.

Hotels (double room with bathroom). Top hotel £120+; middle range hotel £60-80; bed and breakfast £30-40.

Meals and drinks. Dinner for two with wine at a medium-priced restaurant £30-40. Pub lunch for two, with drinks, £10-15. Take-away fish and chips £2.20. Pint of beer £1.50, malt whisky £1.80, bottle of wine in restaurant £8-20, orange juice £1.20. Cup of tea or coffee, 70p-£1.20.

Museum entry. Mostly free.

Petrol. 4-star 64p/litre, unleaded 59p/litre.

Photography. 36-exposure colour transparency film, including pre-paid processing £7.50; 36-exposure colour print film, excluding processing, £4.50.

Sports. Swimming pool admission £1.50; golf-course green fees (Braid Hills course) £6.90; pony-trekking £10 an hour, including use of hard riding hat.

Taxis. 90p flagfall for first 340 yards/60 seconds waiting time; 20p for every subsequent 340 yds/60 seconds. A journey from Waverley Station to the Botanic Garden will cost about £3.4.

Trains. Edinburgh–London return £69 (£44 if booked at least one week in advance); Edinburgh–Glasgow return £12.50 (£7.50 outside peak hours).

Video. One day's hire of a camcorder (one video cassette included) £35; spare video cassettes £5 each.

O

OPENING HOURS

Banks. 9:30 A.M.-4:30 P.M. Monday-Friday.

Museums and art galleries. See page 60.

Post offices. 9:00 A.M.-5:30 P.M. Monday-Friday; 9:00 A.M.-12:30 P.M. Saturday.

Pubs. Generally 11:00 A.M.-1:00 A.M. A few stay open until 2:00 or 3:00 A.M.; on the other hand, some close at 11:00 P.M.

Shops. 9:00 A.M.-5:30 P.M. Monday-Saturday. Many larger shops, and small grocery shops, open on Sunday as well. Large bookshops stay open until 8:00 or 10:00 P.M.

P

PHOTOGRAPHY

Major brands of film are widely available from photo shops, chemists, newsagents, supermarkets, and souvenir shops. Photo shops can process your colour prints in 24 to 48 hours at reasonable prices, and some provide a 1-hour service. Be sure to protect your film from the effects of heat, and never leave a camera or film lying in direct sunlight. Note that the use of flash or tripod is forbidden in a large number of museums and art galleries, so always ask permission before snapping away.

For detailed information on how to get the most out of holiday photographs, purchase a copy of the Berlitz-Nikon Pocket Guide to Travel Photography (available in the U.K. only).

Video. Hand-held video cameras can be hired from the Edinburgh Camcorder Centre, 78 Haymarket Terrace, tel. (0131) 313 5166.

Foreign visitors should make sure that they obtain a camera which is compatible with the system used in their own country. Note also that pre-recorded tapes made for the European market will not play on American equipment.

POLICE (See also EMERGENCIES)

Edinburgh's police officers have a black uniform, and a peaked cap with a black-and-white chequered band. They are not armed, and you will find them friendly and helpful should you have to deal with them. In an emergency, dial 999 and ask for the police.

The headquarters of the Lothian and Borders Police is in Fettes Avenue; for general enquiries, tel. (0131) 311 3131.

Traffic wardens also function in Edinburgh and are merciless about ticketing cars for parking violations.

PUBLIC HOLIDAYS

Most shops and offices, and all banks, will be closed on national public holidays. The other important dates are bank holidays, when in Scotland usually only banks are closed.

If a date falls on a Saturday or Sunday, then the following Monday will be a holiday. In April, May, July, and September there are also four local Edinburgh holiday Mondays, when the majority of shops, banks, and post offices in the city are closed.

In the following list, national public holidays—as opposed to bank holidays—have been indicated by an asterisk (*):

1 January*
2 January*
Good Friday
First Monday in May—Spring Bank Holiday
Last Monday in May—Spring Bank Holiday
First Monday in August—August Bank Holiday
25 December*
26 December

R

RELIGION

The Church of Scotland, which is Presbyterian, is the leading religious denomination in Edinburgh, along with Episcopalian, Methodist, and Roman Catholic congregations.

The city also has a mosque, a synagogue, and an Orthodox church. For details of religious services, tel. (0131) 557 1700

T

TIME DIFFERENCES

The U.K. runs on Greenwich Mean Time (GMT) in winter, and British Summer Time (BST) in summer. The clocks are put forward an hour on the last Saturday in March, and put back again on the last Saturday in October.

The following table shows the time difference in various cities around the world during summer.

Los Angeles	New York	**Edinburgh**	Sydney	Auckland
4:00 A.M.	7:00 A.M.	**noon**	9:00 P.M.	11:00 P.M.

TIPPING

Hotels and restaurants may add a service charge to your bill, in which case there is no need to tip. If service is not included, leave a tip of around 10-15%.

A hotel porter should get around 50p a bag, and a maid about £4-5 a week. Taxi drivers increasingly do not expect a tip, but it is common practice to round the fare up. Tipping is not customary in cinemas, theatres, and petrol stations.

TOILETS/RESTROOMS

There are numerous public toilets conveniently located for tourists visiting Edinburgh's major attractions; nearly all of them are clearly and helpfully signposted.

Handy facilities may be found at Castle Wynd North, below the Esplanade; in Hunter Square on South Bridge; at the foot of the Canongate, opposite the entrance to Holyroodhouse; in the Waverley Market shopping centre; at the Ross Bandstand in Princes Street Gardens; and at Castle Terrace car park. The "Superloos" in Waverley Station have showers as well.

TOURIST INFORMATION OFFICES

The city's main tourist information office is the **Edinburgh and Scotland Information Centre,** situated on top of the Waverley Market shopping centre at the east end of Princes Street.

In addition to providing information on tourist attractions, special events, entertainment, shopping, and restaurants, they provide a same-day or advance booking service for accommodation in Edinburgh, and a book-ahead service for the rest of Scotland; you can even buy tickets for major theatres and concerts, coach tours, walking tours, and certain tourist attractions. There is a currency exchange desk, and a shop selling souvenirs, maps, and books on Edinburgh and Scotland. Tel. (0131) 473 3800.

The Centre is open all year daily 9:00 A.M.-6:00 P.M. (until 7:00 P.M. May, June and September; 8:00 P.M. July and August).

There is also a branch desk at Edinburgh Airport, tel. (0131) 333 2167. Open 8:30 A.M.-9:30 P.M. (from 9:30 A.M. Sundays) April-October; 9:00 A.M.-6:00 P.M. (5:00 P.M. Saturday and Sunday) November-March. Also check the British Arts Cities website at: http://www.bta.org.uk. The Edinburgh Festival website is at www.go edinburgh.co.uk.

You can get information about Edinburgh and Scotland before you leave home by contacting the Scottish Tourist Board, 23 Ravelston Terrace, PO Box 705, Edinburgh EH4 3EU, tel. (0131) 332 2433 (postal and telephone enquiries only), or at one of these offices:

England: Scottish Tourist Board, 19 Cockspur Road, London SW1Y 5BL, tel. (0171) 930 8661.

U.S.A.: British Tourist Authority, 551 West 5th Avenue, 7th Floor, New York NY 10176, tel. (212) 986 2200, (212) 986 2266; fax (212) 986 1188.

British Tourist Authority, 625 North Michigan Avenue, Suite 1510, Chicago IL 60611, tel. (312) 787 0490; fax (312) 787 7746.

Canada: British Tourist Authority, 94 Cumberland Street, Suite 600, Toronto ON M5R 3N3, tel. (416) 925 6326; (888) VISIT UK; fax (416) 961 2175.

South Africa: British Tourist Authority, P.O. Box 6256, JBS Building, 7th Floor, 107 Commissioner Street, Johannesburg 2001, tel. (011) 325 0343; fax (011) 325 0344.

Australia: British Tourist Authority, 171 Clarence Street, Fourth Floor, Sydney, New South Wales 2000, tel. (02) 9377 4400; fax (02) 9377 4499.

TRANSPORT

Edinburgh is a compact city, with most of the main visitor attractions concentrated in the city centre, where walking is easily the most efficient and enjoyable way of getting around. For more out-of-the-way places, there is an excellent bus network.

For information on all kinds of public transport in the Edinburgh region, call Traveline, tel. (0131) 225 3858.

Buses. There are two major bus companies operating in Edinburgh —Lothian Region Transport (LRT), with maroon-and-white buses, and SMT, whose vehicles are green-and-white—plus several smaller, independent operators. Between them they cover the entire city and its surroundings, but tickets bought from one company cannot be used on their competitors' buses.

You buy a ticket from the driver as you enter the bus (keep it until you get off, as an inspector may ask to see it).

Timetables and route information are posted at the main busstops in the city centre. For more detailed information, contact LRT at the Ticket Centre, Waverley Bridge, tel. (0131) 555 6363, or SMT at St. Andrew Square Bus Station, tel. (0131) 663 9233.

Long-distance buses to Glasgow, Inverness, Aberdeen and all other parts of Scotland (and the remainder of the U.K.) depart regularly from St. Andrew Square Bus Station. For details of long-distance fares and timetables, contact Scottish Citylink, (tel.0990 505050) or National Express (tel. 0990 808080).

Taxis. Edinburgh's black cabs operate 24 hours a day. They can be hailed in the street (an illuminated yellow light on the roof means "For Hire"), ordered by telephone, or picked up at one of the many taxi ranks in and around the city centre.

The main ranks are at Waverley and Haymarket railway stations, St. Andrew Square Bus Station, the Caledonian Hotel (west end of Princes Street), the Royal Infirmary (Lauriston Place), and most of the side streets off Princes Street.

Seat belts are fitted in all taxis, and must be worn by law. To order a cab by phone, try Central Radio Cabs, tel. (0131) 229 2468; Radiocabs, tel. (0131) 225 9000; or Capital Castle Taxis, tel. (0131) 228 2555.

Trains. Edinburgh's Waverley Station is a major rail hub, with services to all parts of the U.K. There are numerous local services which are convenient for tourists who want to visit towns in the region, for example North Berwick, Dunbar, Linlithgow, Stirling, St. Andrews and Perth.

Note that Edinburgh has a second main railway station at Haymarket, west of Princes Street. If you are arriving in Edinburgh by train, be sure not to get off at Haymarket by mistake. Waverley is a few minutes further on.

TRAVELLERS with DISABILITIES

Edinburgh is one of Britain's better cities when it comes to provision for people with disabilities. Many public buildings and tourist attractions are wheelchair accessible, and there are also facilities for people with impaired vision and hearing.

Public transport is still a problem, though a large number of taxis are now equipped to carry wheelchairs (look out for a wheelchair symbol on the front of the taxi).

The hilly nature of the city centre can be a problem too, and many streets are too steep to negotiate by wheelchair.

For specific information, and for leaflets detailing access for people with disabilities to hotels, restaurants, public toilets and places of interest, contact the Lothian Coalition of Disabled People, 8 Lochend Road, tel. (0131) 555 2151. For information on accessible transport, call Traveline, tel. (0131) 225 3858.

Edinburgh

Information about the rest of Scotland is provided by Disability Scotland, Princes House, 5 Shandwick Place, Edinburgh EH2 4RG, tel. (0131) 229 8632. All accommodation and sightseeing publications produced by the Scottish Tourist Board include access information.

TRAVELLING TO EDINBURGH (See also AIRPORT)

By air

From the U.K. and Ireland
Edinburgh Airport is served by regular direct flights from Dublin, and from many parts of the U.K., including London Heathrow, London Gatwick, Birmingham, East Midlands, Leeds/Bradford, Cardiff and Belfast.

For information on flights and fares, contact British Airways, tel. 0345 222111; British Midland, tel. (0131) 3443302; Air UK, tel. (0131) 344 3325.

From the U.S.A. and Canada
Scheduled flights: There are as yet no direct scheduled flights from North America to Edinburgh, but there are a number of regular flights from New York, Boston, Washington, Chicago, and Toronto to Glasgow, from where a 90-minute bus or train journey will take you to Edinburgh.

There are also several daily flights to London from all major U.S. and Canadian cities, from where an easy one-hour shuttle flight connects with Edinburgh.

Package tours and charter flights: Finally, there is a selection of package tours and charter flights to Scotland available from certain North American cities. Your travel agent at home will be able to provide further information.

By road
Edinburgh is well-connected by road to the rest of the U.K. There are two main routes from London—via the M1 and M6 motorways, through Birmingham and Manchester, to the A74, then via the A702

to Edinburgh; and via the M1 and A1 through Leeds and Newcastle. The distance from London to Edinburgh is just over 650 km (400 miles); allow 6-8 hours' continuous driving.

There are also good inter-city coach services between London and Edinburgh (see TRANSPORT).

By rail

There is a regular rail service between London and Edinburgh. Trains depart at least hourly in each direction between 6:00 A.M. and 7:00 P.M., and the journey takes between four and five hours; meals and snacks are available on all trains. The London-Edinburgh route is very popular, and reservations are strongly recommended.

For timetable and fares information, tel. (0131) 556 2451; for credit card sales and reservations (Waverley), tel. (0131) 556 5633.

For excursions beyond Edinburgh, tourists can take advantage of a variety of special fare schemes that operate in Scotland. The Freedom of Scotland Travelpass is available for either 8 or 15 consecutive days and gives unlimited travel on Scotland's rail network. It can be purchased at ScotRail stations and selected English travel centres. (Travelpass holders are also able to obtain a 33% reduction on many Scottish bus routes.)

Visitors from abroad who wish to tour by rail can buy a BritRail Pass before leaving their home country. These offer unlimited travel on the rail network throughout Scotland, England, and Wales during a consecutive period of 4, 8, 15, or 22 days, or one month. There is also the Flexipass, allowing journeys to be made on non-consecutive days, for example, 4 days' unlimited travel over an 8-day period. These types of ticket cannnot be purchased within Britain.

W

WATER

Edinburgh's tap water is among the cleanest and best-tasting in Europe. There is no need to resort to expensive bottled mineral water, although it is widely available in grocery stores.

Edinburgh

WEIGHTS and MEASURES

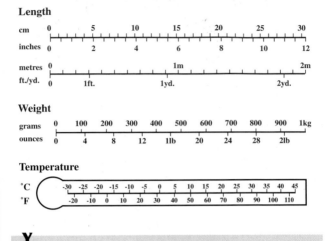

Length

Weight

Temperature

YOUTH HOSTELS

There are two official youth hostels in Edinburgh, run by the Scottish Youth Hostels Association, which can be used by IYHF members—Eglinton Hostel, 18 Eglinton Crescent, tel. (0131) 337 1120, and Bruntsfield Hostel, 7 Bruntsfield Crescent, tel. (0131) 447 2994.

Further information and lists of youth hostels around Edinburgh are available from the following sources:

International Youth Hostel Federation (IYHF), 9 Guessens Road, Welwyn Garden City, Herts AL8 6QW, United Kingdom, tel. (01707) 332 487.

Scottish Youth Hostels Association, 7 Glebe Crescent, Stirling FK8 2JA; tel. (01786) 891400, fax (01786) 891333.

Recommended Hotels

Edinburgh is a major tourist destination, offering a range of accommodation from guest houses to five-star hotels. Around the time of the Festival (August-September) accommodation is at a premium: book as far in advance as possible (a year is not unusual!). The Information Centre (see TOURIST INFORMATION OFFICES) provides a room-finding service. The main hotel/guest house areas are the New Town, West End, and South Side (especially along Newington Road/Mayfield Road).

Listed below is a selection of hotels in four price categories. As a basic guide we have used the symbols below to indicate prices for a double room with bath, including breakfast:

✪✪✪✪	over £120
✪✪✪	£80-120
✪✪	£50-80
✪	below £50

The telephone dialling code for Edinburgh area from outside the city is 0131.

Adam Hotel ✪ *19 Lansdowne Crescent; Tel. 337 1148* Family-run hotel in the West End, just 5 minutes' walk from Princes Street. Its large bedrooms all have televisions. 9 rooms.

Balmoral Hotel ✪✪✪✪ *1 Princes Street EH2 2EQ; Tel. 556 2414, fax 557 8740.* A Princes Street landmark, with distinctive turn-of-the-century architecture and clock tower. Luxury bedrooms, many with fine city views. Indoor pool, sauna, solarium, and gymnasium. 186 rooms.

Bruntsfield Hotel ✪✪✪ *69-74 Bruntsfield Place; Tel. 229 1393, fax 229 5634.* An attractive hotel overlooking the grassy slopes of Bruntsfield Links. Excellent restaurant and two pleasant bars. 50 rooms.

Edinburgh

The Caledonian ✪✪✪✪ *Princes Street EH1 2AB; Tel. 459 9988, fax 225 6632.* "Grand old lady" of Edinburgh hotels, its façade has graced the west end of Princes Street for more than 90 years. Still often rated best in the city. 239 rooms.

Channings ✪✪✪ *South Learmonth Gardens EH4 1EZ; Tel. 315 2225/6, fax 3329631.* 48 rooms, both a brasserie and a hotel made up of five connected town houses. Highly recommended.

Drummond House ✪✪ *17 Drummond Place EH3 6PL; Tel. 557 9189, fax 557-9189.* Delightful little hotel in a Georgian town house only a few minutes away from Princes Street. Friendly reception guaranteed. 4 rooms.

Jarvis Ellersly House ✪✪✪ *4 Ellersly Road EH12 6HI; Tel. 337 6888, fax 313 2543.* Charming Edwardian country house set in its own grounds on the western edge of the city. 57 rooms.

Ellesmere House ✪–✪✪ *11 Glengyle Terrace; Tel. 229 4823, fax 229 5285.* Welcoming guest house in a Victorian terrace overlooking the Meadows, 15 minutes' walk from the Royal Mile. Serves extremely good breakfasts. 6 rooms.

George Inter-Continental ✪✪✪✪ *19-21 George Street EH2 2PB; Tel. 225 1251, fax 226 5644.* A gracious, old-fashioned hotel in the middle of the New Town, with a grand, marble-floored lobby and elegant bedrooms. 195 rooms.

Hilton National ✪✪✪✪ *69 Belford Road EH4 3DG; Tel. 332 2545, fax 332 3805.* Spacious, modern hotel set in a wooded valley beside Water of Leith. Private bathrooms. Excellent restaurant, The Granary, and bar overlooking the river. 144 rooms.

The Howard ✪✪✪✪ *34 Great King Street EH3 6QH; Tel. 557 3500, fax 557 6515.* Friendly hotel in an elegant Georgian terrace, furnished in period style. 10 minutes' walk from Princes Street. Excellent restaurant. 15 rooms.

Iona ✪ *Strathearn Place; Tel. 447 6264, fax 452 8574.* Pleasant family hotel on the city's south side, 10-15 minutes' bus ride from Princes Street. Bar has good pub lunches. 17 rooms.

The Lodge Hotel ✪✪ *6 Hampton Terrace, West Coates EH12 5JD; Tel. 337 3682, fax 313 1700.* Small, family-run hotel in a charming detached villa, about one mile west of the city centre. All 10 rooms have private bathroom and TV. Cocktail bar.

Malmaison ✪✪ *1 Tower Place, Leith EH6 7DB; Tel. 555 6868, fax 555 6999.* Hotel in the restored 19th-century Leith Sailor's Home on the quay; river view. Lively bar and brasserie. 21 rooms.

Murrayfield Park ✪✪ *89 Corstorphine Road; Tel. 337 5370, fax 337 3772.* Close to Murrayfield Stadium, this hotel is always booked well in advance on any rugby match weekend. 23 rooms.

Newington Guest House ✪ *18 Newington Road; Tel. 667 3356.* An attractive, family-run guest house situated on the southern side of the city. It is very conveniently located on the main bus route into the city centre. All the rooms have TV. 8 rooms.

17 Abercromby Place ✪✪ *17 Abercromby Place EH3 6LB; Tel. 557 8036, fax 558 3453.* Exclusive guest house in a Georgian terrace, 5 minutes' walk from Princes Street. Bedrooms and dining room furnished with antiques. 6 rooms.

Norton House ✪✪✪ *Ingliston EH28 8LX; Tel. 333 1275, fax 333 5305.* Country-house hotel set in wooded parkland about 5 miles west of the city centre. Restaurant renowned for its quality menu. 47 rooms.

Roxburghe ✪✪✪ *38 Charlotte Square, Lothian EH2 4HG; Tel. 225 3921, fax 220 2518.* Well-appointed rooms, attentive service: note that rooms overlooking fashionable Charlotte Square may have some traffic noise. 75 rooms.

Recommended Restaurants

Central Edinburgh has numerous excellent restaurants, and there are also many attractive eating places in the country-side around the city. The range of cuisine is wide and enough to satisfy almost every taste; vegetarians are reasonably well catered for (see page 95).

Note that a number of restaurants offer specially priced lunch menus and pre- or post-theatre dinners. Most restaurants are open every day, though some may be closed on Sunday or Monday—it's always worth telephoning to make sure.

Not included below are the attractive cafés at the Scottish National Portrait Gallery and at the Gallery of Modern Art, where you can enjoy a delicious lunch or leisurely afternoon tea. If you find any other places that are worth recommending, we'd be pleased to hear from you.

As an approximate guide we have used the following symbols to give an idea of the price of a three-course meal for two people, excluding drinks. Check your bill to see if a service charge has been included; if not, then it is usual to leave a tip of between 10 and 15%.

✪✪✪	over £40
✪✪	£20-40
✪	below £20

36 ✪ *36 Great King Street; Tel. 556 3636, fax 556 3663.* Located in the basement of a Georgian house only a few minutes' walk from Princes' Street, this establishment specializes in contemporary Scottish cuisine, using the freshest of local ingedients to compose creative meals.

Anna Purna ✪ *45 St. Patrick Square; Tel. 662 1807.* A family-run restaurant serving classic vegetarian dishes from Gujarat and southern India. It offers authentic home cooking, friendly service and pleasant surroundings in which to dine.

Atrium ✪✪✪ *10 Cambridge Street (beside Traverse Theatre;* *Tel. 228 8882, fax 228-8808.* Stylish "designer" restaurant offering an imaginative menu, which changes daily. Accent on seafood and Scottish produce, with everything simply prepared.

Blue Bar Cafe *10 Cambridge Street EH1 2ED; Tel. 221 1222, fax 228 8808.* In the theatre district. Informal high-quality dining. Owned by the proprietors of the Atrium.

Café Royal Oyster Bar ✪✪✪ *17a West Register Street; Tel. 556 4124.* Scotland's oldest seafood restaurant, with an elegant Victorian interior, wood panelling, polished marble, and stained glass. Menu includes game as well as fish, lobster, and oysters. Offers a truly luxurious Sunday brunch.

Chez Jules ✪-✪✪ *Craig's Close (off Cockburn Street); Tel. 225 7007.* A comfortably crowded atmosphere here, and food with a French flavour. Friendly and easy going, a good spot for groups and parties.

Dario's ✪ *85-87 Lothian Road; Tel. 229 9625.* Traditional Italian restaurant offering a wide range of pizza and pasta. The food is nothing special, but the hours are—Dario's stays open until 6 A.M., and is licensed until 5 A.M.

Doric Tavern ✪✪ *15 Market Street; Tel. 225 1084.* An attractive and popular bistro situated just across the street from Waverley Station. A wide-ranging menu draws on French and Oriental influences. Excellent selection of wines.

Drum & Monkey ✪✪ *80 Queen Street; Tel. 538 8111.* Interesting bistro-style place set on the corner below Charlotte Square. The menu mixes traditional Scottish dishes with a touch of French flair—try the black pudding with apple and Calvados chutney. Sunday brunch has to be seen to be believed.

Edinburgh

Dubh Prais Restaurant ✪✪ *123b High Street; Tel. 557 5732.* Relaxed and intimate cellar restaurant down a close off the Royal Mile. Offers fresh Scottish produce—fish, venison, lamb, hare—complemented by simple sauces.

Gordon's Trattoria ✪ *231 High Street; Tel. 225 7992.* There's always a party on here! The waiters join in the fun as they serve up a range of pizzas, pastas and garlic bread. Don't miss the mouth-watering foccacia.

Henderson's Salad Table ✪ *94 Hanover Street; Tel. 225 2131.* A self-service buffet restaurant providing nightly live music. With soups, salad, and a good selection of vegetarian dishes on offer, fresh produce is the order of the day in this inexpensive establishment.

Howie's ✪✪ *63 Dalry Road; Tel. 313 3334.* Bare wood tables and stone floors provide a rustic atmosphere in this Scottish/French restaurant. There is a fixed-price menu that changes every day, but leans towards fresh fish and game.

Marrakech ✪–✪✪ *30 London Street; Tel. 556 7293.* A warm and friendly atmosphere awaits in Edinburgh's only Moroccan restaurant. Exotic specialities include *tajine* (lamb stewed with prunes in a special clay dish) and *couscous* (steamed semolina grains) with a delicious, rich vegetable stew.

Pancho Villa's ✪–✪✪ *240 Canongate; Tel. 557 4416.* Edinburgh's best-value Mexican restaurant. The decor is bright and colourful, the service prompt and cheerful, and the food varied and delicious. Try the deep-fried chillis stuffed with cheese, followed by a sizzling dish of fajitas.

The Rock Restaurant ✪–✪✪ *78 Commercial Street, Commercial Quay; Tel. 555 2225, fax 555 1116.* Located in a fashionable new development in Leith, the cuisine here varies from the famous hamburgers, to international cuisine, to dishes featuring salmon, duck, and other well-loved Scottish ingredients.

Stac Polly ✪✪–✪✪✪ *8-10 Grindlay Street; Tel. 229 5405.* Named after a mountain in the northwest Highlands, Stac Polly brings an imaginative and original approach to traditional Scottish dishes. The roe deer venison and fillet steak are cooked to perfection, and there is even a starter of haggis in filo pastry, with plum and coriander sauce.

Pierre Victoire *10 Victoria Street; Tel. 225 1721.* A French bistro with four other locations in Edinburgh. Very popular, located in the antiques' district. Reservations suggested.

Verandah ✪✪ *17 Dalry Road; Tel. 337 5828.* Comfortable, prize-winning restaurant offering an excellent range of delicious North Indian and Bangladeshi dishes.

Vintners Room ✪✪–✪✪✪ *The Vaults, 87 Giles Street EH6 6BZ; Tel. 554 6767.* An old wine merchants' auction room provides the setting for this intimate, candlelit restaurant. The emphasis is on local produce and dishes, but French cuisine is also on offer.

Waterfront Wine Bar and Bistro ✪✪ *1 Dock Place, Leith, Tel. 554 7427.* One of the leaders in the move to rejuvenate Leith's dockland, this wine bar and bistro is justifiably popular. Its French/Scottish menu is good value, and the setting is marvellous, especially in the lovely conservatory.

The Witchery by the Castle ✪✪✪ *352 Castlehill, Royal Mile; Tel. 225 5613.* Popular restaurant just below the castle, in the heart of the Old Town, serving Scottish fare prepared in French style. The atmospheric original dining room is supposed to be haunted. A second dining room, known as "The Secret Garden," offers another elegant setting.

ABOUT BERLITZ

In 1878 Professor Maximilian Berlitz had a revolutionary idea about making language learning accessible and enjoyable. One hundred and twenty years later these same principles are still successfully at work.

For language instruction, translation and interpretation services, cross-cultural training, study abroad programs, and an array of publishing products and additional services, visit any one of our more than 350 Berlitz Centers in over 40 countries.

Please consult your local telephone directory for the Berlitz Center nearest you or visit our web site at http://www.berlitz.com.

Helping the World Communicate